Cambridge Elements ≡

Elements in Criminology
edited by
David Weisburd
George Mason University
Hebrew University of Jerusalem

LEGITIMACY-BASED POLICING AND THE PROMOTION OF COMMUNITY VITALITY

Tom R. Tyler
Caroline Nobo
Yale Law School

CAMBRIDGE
UNIVERSITY PRESS

CAMBRIDGE
UNIVERSITY PRESS

Shaftesbury Road, Cambridge CB2 8EA, United Kingdom

One Liberty Plaza, 20th Floor, New York, NY 10006, USA

477 Williamstown Road, Port Melbourne, VIC 3207, Australia

314–321, 3rd Floor, Plot 3, Splendor Forum, Jasola District Centre,
New Delhi – 110025, India

103 Penang Road, #05–06/07, Visioncrest Commercial, Singapore 238467

Cambridge University Press is part of Cambridge University Press & Assessment,
a department of the University of Cambridge.

We share the University's mission to contribute to society through the pursuit of
education, learning and research at the highest international levels of excellence.

www.cambridge.org
Information on this title: www.cambridge.org/9781009308045

DOI: 10.1017/9781009308014

First published 2022

A catalogue record for this publication is available from the British Library.

ISBN 978-1-009-30804-5 Paperback
ISSN 2633-3341 (online)
ISSN 2633-3333 (print)

Legitimacy-Based Policing and the Promotion of Community Vitality

Elements in Criminology

DOI: 10.1017/9781009308014
First published online: December 2022

Tom R. Tyler
Caroline Nobo
Yale Law School

Author for correspondence: Tom R. Tyler, tom.tyler@yale.edu

Abstract: This Element presents the history, research, and future potential for an alternative and effective model of policing called "legitimacy-based policing." This model is driven by social psychology theory and informed by research findings showing that legitimacy of the police shapes public acceptance of police decisions, willingness to cooperate with the police, and citizen engagement in communities. Police legitimacy is found to be strongly tied to the level of fairness exercised by police authority, i.e., to procedural justice. Taken together, these two ideas create an alternative framework for policing that relies upon the policed community's willing acceptance of and cooperation with the law. Studies show that this framework is as effective in lowering crime as the traditional carceral paradigm, an approach that relies on the threat or use of force to motivate compliance. It is also more effective in motivating willing cooperation and in encouraging people to engage in their communities in ways that promote social, economic, and political development. We demonstrate that adopting this model benefits police departments and police officers as well as promoting community vitality.

Keywords: harm reduction, legitimacy, procedural justice, evidence-informed policing, community vitality

ISBNs: 9781009308045 (PB), 9781009308014 (OC)
ISSNs: 2633-3341 (online), 2633-3333 (print)

Contents

1 Introduction

The purpose of this Element is to outline a new model of policing that features broader goals and a new set of tactics, discuss the ways in which this model has already been incorporated into discussions of policing, and argue for the benefits of applying this model as a template for twenty-first-century policing, and even expanding its application. As Americans, our own perspective is characterized primarily by the nature of policing in the United States, but we believe that the arguments we make and the model we propose have broad implications for policing in all democratic societies.

Section 2 outlines the features of the coercive model of crime control, which is associated with the threat or use of sanctions. We outline the strengths and weaknesses of this approach. We suggest that as crime has declined, the weaknesses of this model have become more prominent, resulting in the emergence of a reform movement. Two such weaknesses are that the dynamics of coercive policing inevitably produce excesses with respect to the use of force up to and including wrongful shootings, and that coercive policing does not inspire trust in the police on the part of the overall community.

In Section 3, the psychological model of legitimacy-based authority dynamics is presented as a theoretical framework for understanding the exercise of authority in groups, organizations, and societies. The psychological foundations of this broad model are outlined and supportive psychological research from other arenas is presented.

Section 4 uses theories of consent-based authority to articulate a model of legitimacy-based policing. We suggest that this legitimacy-based approach is a better way of addressing the problems of excessive police use of force and low levels of public trust in the police than the coercive model. The adoption of this approach also allows the police to achieve the goal of harm reduction via crime control by enhancing people's willingness to defer to police authority and increasing public cooperation with the police. This model is an effective alternative approach to achieving the long-standing goal of controlling crime through carceral means while avoiding some of the problems associated with that approach. In addition, the model has the advantage of creating a more congenial and constructive relationship between the police and people in the community.

Section 5 explores the ways in which legitimacy-based policing creates a new set of goals for the police with respect to advancing community development, by encouraging residents to identify and engage with their communities. This redefinition of policing establishes a new mission for police, one that is particularly relevant in an era of relatively low crime levels. It highlights a desirable role for local police in the form of a police service that is not focused on crime control. Research suggests that legitimacy-based policing can both achieve traditional goals associated with controlling crime and promote community development.

Section 6 focuses on the potential for expanding the model of procedural justice to include the role of community input in decisions regarding the management of community problems, including but not limited to problems related to crime. The legitimacy-based model emphasizes the idea that it is important to consider community input in decisions about how the community should be policed, as well as in decisions about particular policing policies and practices.

Three issues must be addressed. The first pertains to identifying what people in the community indicate that they want and need. What are the problems they face, and how should these be solved? Second, some type of deliberative procedure must be developed to reach community consensus regarding shared needs and goals. In this context, the focus on procedures that are responsive to community views can be extended beyond the level of policy implementation to that of policy creation, with people in the community becoming increasingly involved in the task of defining the features of a safe and desirable community. This shift includes the task of identifying models to support the coproduction of a community agenda that addresses safety issues and defines the most desirable role for the police. Procedural justice is a natural framework for exploring policy creation because the procedural justice model asks community members about their goals and how they would like those goals to be achieved. The final issue refers to the need to develop procedures for combining the expertise of outside stakeholders (e.g., government authorities, researchers, and the police) with the views of people within the community. Community views cannot simply dictate what happens because the public frequently operates without information and in response to moral panics. On the other hand, decisions cannot simply reflect the preferences of "experts," with community concerns merely sidelined and ignored.

1.1 Goals of This Element

This Element is not a meta-analysis, and it is not our intention to conduct a systematic empirical evaluation of the arguments associated with the model (several excellent meta-analyses already exist, including an overview of the relevant literature in a recent National Academy of Sciences report on proactive policing, i.e., Weisburd & Majmundar, 2018). Instead, we will use selected studies from the field to illustrate the nature of research contributions to this area. Our view is that our primary contribution is the development of an alternative conceptual framework within which policing can be organized and the presentation of evidence that this model can work. Recent evidence in criminological scholarship suggests that this framework has gained considerable traction in the academic literature concerning the police (Farrington, Cohn, & Skinner, 2022). Our focus in this Element is its impact upon police policies and practices.

Our shared belief is that the reform of criminal law is at a pivotal threshold, and our desire is to draw upon these reform efforts to promote evidence-based theories and the policies and practices that they support to identify desirable directions for American policing in the twenty-first century. This Element summarizes our perspective on the reasons why the ideas of legitimacy and procedural justice have been utilized in the academic literature concerning policing, their potential implications for policing policies and practices, and our grounds for believing that they have continuing relevance for scholars and practitioners in this arena both today and in the future.

In addition, we believe that recent developments demonstrate two ideas. The first pertains to the value of theories in the social sciences for criminology and the development of policies in criminal law. The theoretical models and empirical studies pertaining to legitimacy and procedural justice–based policing policies have contributed to discussions concerning twenty-first-century American policing. The second idea highlights the importance of evidence-based policy. Criminologists emphasize the benefits that can result from basing policies on evidence (Weisburd & Neyroud, 2011), and research concerning legitimacy-based policing is one example of these benefits.

2 The Coercive Model of Crime Suppression: Sanction-Based Harm Reduction

What are the elements of the coercive model of policing? The goal of the coercive model is to lower the rate of crime, especially violent crime, i.e., to maximize harm reduction. The strategy employed to achieve this goal is to project police presence into the community to increase the perceived risk of being caught and sanctioned for breaking the law. This approach has been the primary model of policing used in recent decades. It is sometimes referred to as the carceral model because it is based on the threat or use of punishment and incorporates a coercive dynamic. A set of practices pertaining to social control or deterrence ensures the dominance of police over people and situations to guarantee compliance.

Why did this model of policing develop in the United States? A key factor in this process was the dramatic increase in violent crime that occurred throughout America between 1960 and 1990. During that period, FBI crime reports indicate that violent crime increased from less than 200 offenses per 100,000 people to more than 750 cases per 100,000 people per year. This increase in crime was accompanied by a wave of both fear of crime victimization and concerns regarding the damaging impacts of crime and disorder on American cities.

The police reacted to this "crime wave" by recourse to the dominant model in law, i.e., the economic model of the person, whose application to criminal legal processes was pioneered by Becker (1968). This model argues that crime is deterred by the threat or use of sanctions. To implement this model, police departments increased their numbers and deployed additional resources to accomplish the goal of suppressing crime via the surveillance of communities and the apprehension of criminals. This "command-and-control" approach became central to policing, but it also dominated the policies and practices of the courts and correctional institutions. The approach relies on the capacity of the police to effectively shape public behavior using a strategy of projecting the potential or real use of force.

A strategy based on force encourages and supports a culture based on a warrior style of policing according to which officers are concerned with their capacity to utilize coercive measures, leading to their deployment with a variety of weapons and extensive training in their use. As police officers are given the legal right to use force, their training and culture concurrently emphasizes ways of using force effectively.

2.1 Evaluating the Strength of Harm Reduction Models

There are three positive aspects of policing goals and strategy under this coercive approach. First, the police became more proactive. They focused on preventing crime rather than merely reacting to crimes. Such a proactive orientation is a key strategy for harm reduction, and its purpose is to prevent damaging events that harm people and undermine communities. Today, police chiefs are held accountable for the crime rates in their jurisdictions irrespective of whether they retroactively catch and punish those who commit crimes. As a result, the police implemented enhanced policies for intervening in advance to intercept criminals, a shift which led to a series of increasingly broad policies regarding police-initiated investigatory contact with people in the community with the aim of preempting future criminal activity. As an example, a knife or gun taken from someone on the street cannot be used to commit a crime in the future. Similarly, a person who fears police searches may not carry a gun.

Second, during the period 1960–90, the police developed their practices on the foundation of theories concerning ways of addressing crime. As noted, one key theory is the economic theory–based deterrence model, which suggests that projecting force increases the perceived risk of committing a crime and thereby lowers the rate of crime.

A second theory referenced by the police is the broken windows theory. The broken windows theory is based on research in the social sciences, particularly on research conducted by the social psychologist Zimbardo (1969). Kelling and Wilson (1982) draw upon these studies to develop an evidence-informed approach to managing crime and disorder (Keizer, Lindenberg, & Steg, 2008). The proactive policing strategy is based on theoretical arguments associated with the broken windows model. According to that model, a consistent path leads from minor crimes to serious crimes. On an individual level, people who commit minor crimes go on to commit serious crime, so interventions that address minor crimes are a preventative strategy.

At the community level, if minor crimes are left unaddressed, a general deterioration in the quality of neighborhoods takes place, which also promotes serious crime (Lanfear, Matsueda, & Beach, 2020; O'Brien, Farrell, & Welsh, 2019). Hence, a key assumption underlying approaches to policing has been the belief that by addressing minor crimes, the police are able to prevent major crimes in the future. An example of this dynamic is the widespread pattern of arresting individuals for marijuana possession. While minor drug possession or drinking beer in a park are crimes, the justification for police focusing on these crimes is that, if left unaddressed, they are a prelude to more serious criminal activity. Similarly, allowing everyday disorder to go unchecked leads to community decline.

Third, the police implemented the idea of identifying and utilizing empirical metrics to assess their success. This shift is reflected in the widely emulated COMPSTAT model developed and used in New York City. That model is used to adjust policies and practices in accordance with rapid assessments of the crime rate in different localities. This approach involves gathering ongoing data and using these empirical metrics to guide police deployment in real time. In this case, the police typically use a neighborhood-based metric of crime rates. The key to this metric is collecting data that are sufficiently geographically specific to be tactically useful and having access to such data in real time.

2.2 The Warrior Culture

How have police departments organized themselves to implement these models of crime control? As a reaction to the mission of crime control on the basis of deterrence, police departments have widely adopted a warrior culture. The sanction-based model requires the police to project force and to be willing to use the threat of force to ensure compliance. Police officers are trained in the use of force to compel compliance and are equipped with a variety of weapons to support that approach. This leads to a culture focused on the capacity to deploy force to create a climate of dominance over people and situations.

The consequence of the widespread adoption of the coercive model is that the police in contemporary America are generally trained in one primary model and equipped to employ one primary skill set. They learn how to use force to compel obedience. They apply this command-and-control framework to the broad range of problems they encounter because it is the central tool in their toolkit of strategies for dealing with issues in the community. Of course, there exist individual officers who employ other types of social skills in their work or receive some form of de-escalation or empathy training; however, the common feature of policing in America is a focus on using or threatening to use force to compel compliance from members of the public.

Frequently, the threat of force is implied, with officers carrying clubs, mace, tasers, and guns to make their capacity to use force salient to whomever they encounter. In other cases, the threat is overt, with officers threatening violence when speaking to members of the community or using physical force. The policing model is based on dominating people and situations via the implied or explicit use of force.

How frequent are such behaviors? Based on his study of policing in Indianapolis and St. Petersburg, Terrill (2001, p. 223) suggests that "nearly 60% of the observed police–citizen encounters [he reviewed] involved some form of force" and that 15.7 percent of these encounters escalated beyond verbal pressure to physical force (Terrill 2001, p. 88). Terrill further suggests that 20 percent of the cases in which force is used feature a nonresistant person. Similarly, MacDonald et al. (2003) report that the use of force is most frequent when police are confronted with nonthreatening situations. A national survey conducted in 2018 suggests that when Black Americans report on their most recent experiences with the police, they indicate that the police used intimidating language 19 percent of the time, threatened force 13 percent of the time, and handcuffed them 16 percent of the time. Among these same respondents, 25 percent report that the use of intimidating language is frequent in their neighborhood; 26 percent report that the police frequently use threats of force; and 30 percent report that the police bully or intimidate people (Goff & Tyler, 2018).

It might seem as if the use of force is a necessary component of a strategy that is designed to ensure compliance. It is therefore important to note that this warrior style is not necessarily more effective in achieving the goal of compelling compliance (McCluskey, Mastrofski, & Parks, 1999). McCluskey notes that "the coercive power that police bring to bear on a citizen in the form of commanding, handcuffing, arresting and so on, has a minimal impact on citizen's compliance decisions" (McCluskey, 2003, p. 100). Why? Because "for every one unit increase [in] the index of coercion citizens are about twice as likely to rebel against the self-control request" (McCluskey, 2003, p. 108). He notes that higher levels of coercive action lead to a lower likelihood of compliance.

2.3 Declines in Crime in the United States

One reason for the adoption and continued use of a force-based model of policing is that this strategy seems to have been successful. Since the 1990s, crime rates have consistently decreased. This decline has been long-term and sustained. At present, the crime rate is much lower than it was in 1980. If we consider the rates of two representative crimes – murder and burglary – it becomes apparent that there was a peak in crimes around 1980 and that the present crime rate has decreased to levels far below those reported in the 1960s. This claim holds true across major cities, and even cities such as Chicago that continue to receive media attention for violent crimes have much lower rates of crime than they did in the 1980s. At present, crime is dramatically rarer than it was during the 1980s (Gramlich, 2020). In the context of ongoing discussions regarding whether crime increased or decreased due to COVID-19, it is important to recognize that, over time and across communities, striking and sustained decreases in the rate of crime have occurred. Even recent COVID-19-related increases in crime have not altered this basic point (Abt, Bocanegra, & Tingirides, 2022).

It is also important to note that while the crime rate is at a historically low level, crime rates remain viable as a political argument in discussions regarding policing. This viability is reflected in discussions concerning recent COVID-19-related increases in crime. These rises, although small, have focused on the police as the figures who suppress crime and calm public fears. A consequence of this shift is that public opinion polls suggest increasing support for the police (Parker & Hurst, 2021). In 2020, 31 percent of the population supported greater funding for the police, while, in 2021, 47 percent supported greater funding. Why? In 2021, 61 percent indicated that violent crime is a very serious problem in the country, an increase from 41 percent in 2020.[1]

---

[1] It is important to distinguish short-term changes from long-term trends. Analyses of the General Social Survey from 1986–2018 suggest steady increases in the percentage of Americans who indicate that there is too much spending on law enforcement (Roscigno & Preito-Hodge, 2021).

As noted, the public increasingly holds the police responsible for preventing crime, so irrespective of actual crime rates, if the public believes that crime is a problem, addressing crime is an important issue that affects police support from the community. Hence, decreases in crime rates constitute an important justification for police departments' policies and practices. The police are important, but the decrease in crime rates is the result of a combined effort on the part of the police, private security forces, and community groups as well as of changing social and economic conditions and demographic shifts over time.

Declining crime rates do not justify all aspects of proactive policing. The widespread use of investigatory stops to preempt crimes, occasionally known as a policy of "stop, question, and frisk," has not been found by researchers to have a strong impact on crime rates (Weisburd & Majmundar, 2018). Some evidence suggests that some police tactics can be effective, e.g., the policing of hotspots, but other evidence suggests that some widely used tactics are not effective (Braga & Weisburd, 2010). This claim is not unique to policing. The use of long-term prison sentences to control crime has also been found to have a minimal impact on crime rates (Kleiman, 2009).

2.4 Problems Associated with Force-Based Policing

Since crime has declined, it is reasonable to ask why people would argue that there is a need to change policing. On the surface, it would seem that the police have engaged in a successful effort to reduce harm.

The current policing model faces several problems that have led to arguments for reform, even in the face of apparent success. One such problem is that the warrior style of policing has a dynamic that encourages the unnecessary use of force. It is possible to view some instances of the excessive use of force as the result of a few bad actors, and the legal system's response to this situation encourages such a response by retroactively evaluating the legality of the actions of individual officers. Many of the reforms that have achieved national visibility are aimed at managing a small subset of problematic officers. One example of such a reform is the implementation of a national database of previously sanctioned officers.

An organizational analysis suggests that these instances of the excessive use of force are a natural extension of the warrior style of policing. Recognition that the style of policing frames the actions of police officers is important because such recognition makes it clear that these instances of excessive use of force can best be understood not as aberrations but rather as the foreseeable results of the skill set that the police deploy in the situations they encounter in their communities. Lethal instances of the use of force, as noted, make the headlines, but it is the underlying social dynamics that produce these cases that must be addressed in an effort to reduce the excessive use of force (Camp et al., 2021).

Declining crime has exacerbated the problems associated with police use of force because it has changed the kind of problems the police encounter most frequently. Being prepared to use force to compel compliance has never been a skill set that is well suited to the actions the police take in their everyday duties. Quattlebaum and Tyler (2020) review the literature concerning police tasks and conclude that approximately 4 percent of the tasks the police perform on a daily basis require the capacity to deploy force to compel compliance. A recent analysis by Lum, Koper, and Wu (2021) focused on responses to calls to the police suggests that only approximately 9 percent of the time spent responding to calls involves issues associated with violence. Lum and colleagues (2021) report that the police perform a wide variety of services within their communities, most of which are unrelated to the need to compel obedience via the threat or use of force. And Parks et al. (1999) report that the police spend only approximately 25 percent of an average day investigating crimes or apprehending criminals. Furthermore, Webster (1970) suggests that patrol officers spend less than 3 percent of their time on dispatches related to crimes against persons.

The reality of policing is that the police provide a variety of social services. Although municipal social service budgets have been reduced, requests for such services have increased. Accordingly, a continually increasing proportion of the issues that the police address are unconnected to controlling crime and do not require the capacity to deploy force. Consequently, the police are increasingly poorly trained to perform the tasks they are required to carry out on a daily basis.

Terrill, Rossler, and Paoline III (2014) examine the content of police interactions in three cities (Flint, Indianapolis, and St. Petersburg), dividing them into requests for assistance that involve problem-solving and requests that involve controlling other people (e.g., by arresting them). These authors found that 58 percent of police encounters involve problem-solving. As another author notes, "It is unfortunate for the country that the police are imbued with this totally wrong perception of themselves. The police do perform social work. In fact, they perform more social work than they perform law enforcement. Regretfully, as social workers, most police are poorly trained and incompetent" (Webster, 1970, p. 100).

One type of social service involves responding to requests for help, whether in person, via 911 (emergency) calls, or using other forms of communication that are rapidly proliferating (email, social media platforms, etc.). The role played by the police in responding to local problems is intentional, since many police departments have developed 911 centers that channel public problems to the police to receive a response. As a result, "dispatched calls represent the most common police mobilization" (Terrill, Rossler, & Paoline III, 2014, p. 493).

From the perspective of a warrior culture, providing such assistance is inconsistent with "real policing," especially when it involves dealing with minor everyday neighborhood problems. Such efforts are occasionally disparaged as "social work" as distinct from efforts to suppress crime. Hence, one limitation of the coercive crime control model is that it promotes a skill set that is suitable only for a small set of police activities, and the frequency of these activities is declining. As crime declines, the police engage in more social service activities, and the mismatch between these activities and their skills increases.

The current model of policing inevitably produces problems associated with excessive force. These reflect the underlying reality of the mismatch between tasks and skills. Even if the police never shot anyone, their skill set would exacerbate community issues in two ways: First, they define interactions that do not require the threat or use of force as issues of control and dominance, thus provoking conflict spirals; and, second, they fail to develop the type of social skills that would be helpful in managing the problems the police encounter most frequently.

A second problem is that the current style of policing is not conducive to building trust. The 2004 National Academy of Sciences report on policing (Skogan & Frydl, 2004) notes that the police have generally become more professional and lawful, while their efforts have facilitated decreases in crime rates. Despite these successes, public trust in the police has not increased: It has been found by national surveys to range between 50 and 60 percent for decades and has not risen as crime has declined. In fact, trust in the police has not changed substantially since 1980 (Tyler, Goff, & MacCoun, 2015). Public opinion surveys indicate that a substantial number of Americans have distrusted and continue to distrust their local police departments and that this distrust is much higher in minority communities. A recent Gallup poll indicates that approximately 50 percent of adult Americans express distrust in their local police departments (Brenan, 2021a). It is striking that, despite living in a democratic society, half of the people in America do not trust their local police force. Moreover, trust among minority Americans is much lower. In the Gallup poll mentioned above, trust was found to be 29 percent lower among minority Americans than among White Americans. This situation highlights the paradox of decreasing crime rates and increasing levels of police professionalism (Sklansky, 2014), yet with no upturn in public trust.

If crime rates have decreased, does it matter if people trust their local police? There are several reasons to think that this factor might be important. First, trust lowers criminal activity, so research suggests that if the police were more highly trusted, crime rates would decrease further (Tyler, 2006b). By failing to raise trust, the police are neglecting one of the motivations for avoiding the commission of crimes – viewing law as legitimate – with respect to their strategies aimed at controlling crime.

Furthermore, a frequent complaint expressed by the police is that people in the community do not help them by reporting crimes or identifying criminals. Distrust undermines cooperation, while trust promotes it. The problems associated with distrust include low clearance rates, unwillingness to testify in court, disinterest in joining a community watch or neighborhood patrol, and even supporting the acquittal of criminal defendants due to the belief that police officers lie when testifying or because of a desire to nullify laws. Low trust undermines police efforts to control crime.

Ironically, this lack of trust reinforces the need for a warrior model of policing. If the goal of the police is to ensure compliance, officers must ask how it can be guaranteed. One approach would be to appeal to their legitimate authority. However, if the police lack legitimacy in the eyes of the people they encounter, officers can always default to the use of force to direct public behavior. Most likely, they make this assumption prior to engaging with people, since studies suggest that they typically project dominance immediately in encounters rather than as a reaction to the actions of the civilian (Voigt et al., 2017). As noted, this approach further undermines public trust and enhances the need to utilize force once again in the future.

It is important to emphasize the ways in which an approach focused on the use of the force can push policing in the direction of a spiral of conflict. As the police undermine their legitimacy, they increasingly require the use of force to do their job. This use of force, in turn, promotes anger and resistance and further undermines trust. In any given moment, it may seem to police officers that they have little alternative but to use force irrespective of its downstream consequences. However, research disputes this approach and suggests that even people who are highly mistrustful of the police react favorably to fair treatment and, in particular, to interpersonal respect. It is never too late for the police to begin reversing the social dynamics of distrust. However, the coercive approach undermines such efforts.

Lack of trust also reinforces the danger imperative mindset among police officers (Sierra-Arévalo, 2021). Officers perceive themselves as living in a dangerous world, surrounded by risks and facing a hostile population. It is easy to see why they might feel this way, since a force-based approach, when combined with wide-ranging preemptive investigatory stops, causes the police to come into frequent contact with angry community residents and to encounter many situations in which interactions lead to various levels of conflict. Parks and colleagues (1999), for example, estimate that 30 percent of police contacts involve some form of resistance, pushback, or conflict. The perception of risk that officers feel regarding their own safety becomes a self-fulfilling prophecy when officers approach interactions in a self-protective manner, for example, with guns drawn, which communicates suspicion and distrust that fuels hostility and backlash, thereby creating more risk of conflict (Kirkpatrick et al., 2021).[2]

Finally, the failure of the police to develop trust causes policing to be a self-perpetuating phenomenon. Since people do not view the law and legal authority as legitimate, a continuing police presence is necessary to motivate compliance and suppress crime. Yet that presence does not develop trust, so the police are always necessary. The current model of policing, in other words, has no endgame. It is not based on the idea of developing the public's capacity or motivation to take personal responsibility for rule following. It is a crime suppression model, and suppression requires the ongoing presence of the threatened or actual use of force. Suppression is aimed at producing immediate changes in behavior and, to the degree that it has a long-term impact on behavior, it increases the likelihood of future criminality by crowding out the internal motivations that support rule-following behavior.

2.5 Legitimacy-Based Policing

Several problems with the way existing policing is organized have been noted. The first problem is that the use of the force model inevitably leads to the excessive use of force. In addition, force is mismatched with the tasks that the police perform, a problem that has exacerbated as crime rates have declined and the need for social services has risen. Further, current styles of policing do not develop public trust and consequently do not encourage people to defer to police discretion regarding how to exercise authority and/or willingly cooperate with the police. Recognition of these limitations gave rise to the police reform movement, as discussed in the following section.

3 Psychological Models of Authority

The policing community became concerned about public trust in the early twenty-first century in the wake of declining crime rates. As noted, the question

---

[2] Studies of interpersonal interactions suggest that people who approach them with the goal of controlling or dominating provoke similar behavior in others, even those who might otherwise be inclined to be cooperative. As a consequence, they are always dealing with hostile opponents and come to believe that everyone is hostile; they typically fail to see that others' behavior is provoked by their own actions (Kelley & Stahelski, 1970).

of why such declines did not lead to heightened public support for the police was raised by a series of high profile instances in which the police were viewed as abusive or as misusing force. In this context, it became clear that a substantial minority of the public is mistrustful of the police, unwilling to defer to their authority, and willing to support police reform.

When legitimacy became an issue in policing, police scholars sought a framework for addressing this issue. Because police scholarship, like policing itself, had focused extensively on issues of legality and performance, the literature was sparse. Consequently, psychologists were drawn into discussions within the policing community.

Commonly, in the case of reform efforts based on moments of crisis, public leaders search for literature that they can reference to provide short-term solutions to their concerns. In recent years, the psychological literature pertaining to legitimacy has seemed to be most relevant to concerns about policing. This focus explains why these streams of literature have been referenced by criminology scholarship and helps illuminate why, once drawn into the framework of that literature, these ideas do not always translate seamlessly, particularly in methodological terms. The efforts of police leaders to employ this framework to develop policies were faster than the development of a separate empirical literature in the context of policing.

3.1 The Psychology of Authority

The psychological literature concerning legitimacy draws on four distinct streams of psychological theory and research related to the dynamics of authority in groups, organizations, communities, and societies: (1) legitimacy; (2) procedural justice; (3) social exchange; and (4) social identity. None of these streams of literature was initially developed to feature a focus on policing or even law more generally. Rather, each represents a general psychological model that addresses all social interactions that involve some form of authority. Within this framework, legitimacy is a goal, procedural justice is a strategy for achieving that goal, and social exchange and social identity address the reasons people care about the justice of the procedures used by authorities. Of these ideas, procedural justice has achieved the most prominence in social science scholarship. Hagan and Hans (2017) noted over 30,000 references to work pertaining to procedural justice in Google Scholar citations in the five years before their review. During the period 2019–21, there were 16,800 such references.

The four streams of literature are drawn together in *Why People Obey the Law* (Tyler, 1990, 2006b), where they are used as a framework for research concerning the reasons why people comply with the law in their everyday lives as well as the ways in which they experience personal interactions with police officers and courts. In a subsequent volume, *Trust in the Law* (Tyler & Huo, 2002), the same framework is used to examine the reasons why people defer to the decisions made by judges and police officers.

This literature reflects the contributions of several leading social psychological theorists and researchers. In the case of legitimacy, Kurt Lewin pioneered research in this arena, and Stanley Milgram and Herbert Kelman later contributed. Procedural justice developed out of the general social psychological literature concerning social justice (Tyler et al., 1997) and was highlighted by Thibaut and Walker (1975) and Leventhal (1980). The social exchange literature reflects the work of Thibaut and Kelley (1959). Finally, social identity theories reflect the work of both European scholars such as Tajfel and Turner (1986) and Americans (for example, Leary, 2007).

3.1.1 Legitimacy

Psychology articulates a view of people's relationship to authority that puts emphasis on what is going on in their minds. In particular, it suggests that people develop long-term dispositions that separate their evaluations and behaviors from their responsiveness to immediate environmental circumstances. Legitimacy is concerned with feelings of obligation and responsibility to defer to authorities. This factor is particularly valuable to authority because when people feel that an authority is legitimate they authorize that authority to make decisions regarding appropriate behavior for themselves and others, and they feel an obligation to follow those decisions. For the followers, this obligation requires them to do what an authority figure tells them to do. For the authorities, it causes them to feel entitled to tell the followers how to behave (i.e., to feel self-legitimacy).

The empirical study of perceived or subjective legitimacy is a post–World War II phenomenon in psychology that is associated with Kurt Lewin. World War II demonstrated the centrality of social dynamics to the nature of societies (see Lewin, Lippitt, & White, 1939). The work of Lewin and associates concerning the dynamics of authority both demonstrates the influence of legitimacy acquired by a democratic leadership style on people's willingness to accept the recommendations of authorities and highlights the important role that democratic governance plays in the creation and maintenance of legitimacy (Gold, 1999).[3]

---

[3] The work of Lewin is important because it represents an effort to study the influence of legitimacy empirically. The classic empirical study in this field is Lewin et al. (1939). This study does not mention the term legitimacy, nor is it focused explicitly on issues of rule following. Nonetheless, it constructs the psychological framework within which issues pertaining to the legitimacy of authority have been subsequently addressed in social psychology.

Lewin showed that a democratic leadership style promotes a willing commitment toward performing group tasks that is not linked to the presence of an authority (i.e., members' have internal motivation). This situation causes group members to want to pursue group goals. The key elements of this work can be found in modern psychology: a procedurally just style of authority (that gives people a voice and allows discussion) causes an authority to be legitimate. Such legitimacy motivates group members to act voluntarily to pursue group goals. This internal motivation leads group members to act in the interests of the group irrespective of personal rewards and sanctions associated with the situation. In Lewin's studies, democratically led groups engaged in group tasks irrespective of whether an authority figure was present, while autocratically led groups stopped working if the leader left the room.

The concept of legitimacy has continued to play a role in social psychology since this early work. In a classic paper, French Jr. and Raven (1959) identify legitimacy as one of the five bases of social power. Simultaneously, it would not be correct to describe the legitimacy of authorities as a central focus of theory or research in psychology. The idea of internal vs. external motivation has been the most important contribution of this early work rather than a focus on legitimacy. The study of the legitimacy of authority has been more prominent in other social sciences (Tyler, 2006a).

In the field of psychology, the classic study examining legitimacy is the Milgram obedience to authority study (Milgram, 1975). This focuses on when and why people obey authorities. Milgram's research concerning deference to authority demonstrates the powerful influence of directives from an authority figure on behavior (Milgram, 1975). Milgram shows that people are willing to take action, in this case delivering shocks to others, when told to do so by an authority figure they view as legitimate.

Like Lewin, Milgram does not directly measure legitimacy; rather, his work demonstrates the power of authority. Moreover, like Lewin, he manipulates situations in ways that, he suggests, reflect variations in legitimacy – for example, the scientific status of the authority or the standing of the educational institution within which the study occurs. The legitimacy of the experimenter and the research setting determine whether participants willingly suspend their own judgment and follow the directives issued by the authority figure. These studies demonstrate to psychologists the powerful role that legitimacy can play in shaping behavior.

Referring to legitimacy as "authorization," Kelman and Hamilton (1989, p. 16) argue that when an authority is legitimate, "the duty to obey superior orders" replaces personal morality and people allow legitimate authorities to define the boundaries of appropriate behavior in a given situation. An authority figure can authorize people to engage in a behavior so that they substitute their feelings of being obligated to obey for their personal judgments concerning self-interest or morality. For this reason, the possession of legitimacy gives authorities power over the behavior of others. Such power can have positive consequences, as when people defer to authorities in the context of resolving disputes, or it can have negative social consequences, as when people follow directives to harm others (Kelman & Hamilton, 1989; Milgram, 1975).

3.1.2 Procedural Justice

Social psychology made another important theoretical contribution by highlighting the concept of social justice. This emphasis led to the development of several important streams of psychological literature focused on distributive, procedural, and retributive justice. In the 1980s, distributive justice principles such as equity became the primary focus of justice research. Psychologists then isolated the separate idea of procedural justice. Leventhal (1980) explicitly titled his article "What should be done with equity theory?" [4] At approximately the same time, the social psychologist John Thibaut collaborated with law professor Laurens Walker to develop a model of procedural justice (Thibaut & Walker, 1975).

The basic idea of procedural justice is that people have normative models concerning the way in which they believe authority should be exercised. When they interact with third party authorities, they evaluate those authorities in terms of whether they act in ways that are consistent with these models. This evaluation is distinct from their views concerning the favorability or fairness of their outcomes when dealing with that authority, as well as from broader assessments of lawfulness or competence. People make these judgments as a reaction to their personal contacts and when they encounter the overall operation of some system of authority. On a theoretical level, these ideas apply to any type of authority: parents, teachers, managers, police officers, judges, prison guards, administrative judges, mediators, etc.

The primary way in which the notion of procedural justice was introduced to the field of legal psychology was the seminal book *Procedural justice: A psychological analysis* (Thibaut & Walker, 1975). This book tests a procedural justice model of authority in a trial setting. As noted, procedural justice theories need not be formulated in terms pertaining to law or legal authority, although the field of law contains a large number of studies pertaining to procedure; so this marriage of social justice models in a legal trial setting is important with respect to the subsequent influence of procedural justice in law.

---

[4] Equity is one form of distributive justice.

The study of procedural justice emerged as a substantial force due to the experimental studies of Thibaut and his graduate students (see Lind & Tyler, 1988).

While the Thibaut and Walker (1975) book is wide-ranging, one issue for which it does not provide empirical support is the antecedent factors that shape legitimacy. Disputants' satisfaction with a verdict is influenced by procedure. Participants' trust in judges is not found to be influenced. This work establishes that disputants' satisfaction with trial verdicts is influenced by the fairness of the procedures used in the trial in question, which is distinct from the favorability of the outcome. Similarly, Leventhal does not articulate a theory of authority as part of his procedural justice model and does not focus on legitimacy.

The procedural justice literature provides an answer to the question of how legitimacy can be created and maintained. If authorities exercise their authority via just procedures, they can improve satisfaction with those procedures in a manner that is distinct from their outcomes. Of course, as noted, the link to authorities is not clear in this early research. Tyler and Caine (1981) provide evidence of such an extension in a set of studies concerning the legitimacy of authorities that directly connects the latter to their use of procedural justice.

Over time, procedural justice has developed to incorporate four aspects of the exercise of authority (Blader & Tyler, 2003). These elements are not derived from philosophical speculation. Rather, empirical studies show that these four aspects are the factors that people consider when they decide whether the procedures being used are just.

Two elements of procedural justice are related to decision-making. First, people want a voice. They want the relevant authority to allow them to express their views or tell their side of the story before developing policies or making decisions. Second, people care about neutrality. They want authorities to act in a transparent and impartial manner by making decisions based upon facts rather than prejudices. Neutrality is also related to whether the authorities explain what their policies are and how they are being applied and apply them consistently over time and across the people with whom they deal.

Next, two elements pertaining to procedural justice are related to interpersonal treatment. First, people want interpersonal respect, courtesy, and politeness. This term includes respect for people's rights as citizens and for their dignity as people. People care about whether the authorities treat them in ways that indicate that they are viewed as good citizens rather than suspects, deviants, or marginal members of their community (Tyler, Jackson, & Mentovich, 2015). Second, they are concerned with whether the authorities' actions are based on trustworthy motives. It is important for people to feel that the authorities are motivated to do what is good for the people in their communities. They want to believe that the authorities are sincere and benevolent, focused on the needs and goals of the parties, and willing to acknowledge and address people's concerns.

These four elements, i.e., voice, neutrality, respect, and trust, are central to public judgments concerning how fairly legal authority is exercised in the community, as well as to people's personal experiences with legal authorities. While these elements are consistently found to be relevant, the relative importance of these elements varies across situations (Barrett-Howard & Tyler, 1986). Other elements can be important in particular settings and, under some conditions, concerns regarding outcome fairness or even outcome favorability become more influential.

3.1.3 Social Exchange

The history of social psychology is centered on models of social exchange that view people as motivated to maximize personal gains and avoid losses when interacting with others. Does procedural justice represent a distinct model of authority? Interestingly, while they support the idea of procedural justice, Thibaut and Walker (1975) advocate an instrumental model of justice. They suggest that people use fair procedures to achieve desired outcomes. They are not driven by some distinct motive pertaining to justice. In the view of these authors, fair procedures are a means of obtaining good outcomes. An example of this phenomenon is the idea of voice. From an instrumental perspective, people want to present evidence and state their case to increase their likelihood of winning and receiving what they want.

3.1.4 Social Identity

A key question in the literature pertains to whether there are noninstrumental reasons for wanting procedural justice. An important set of motives identified by social psychologists refers to people's identities and feelings of self-worth. At the individual level, people want to be respected and valued by others to maintain a positive self-image. At the group level, they want to be members of groups that have high status (inclusion), and they want to have status within those groups (standing). Authorities who speak for groups can communicate status and standing, thus facilitating high self-esteem and a positive identity. All these theories represent variations on the theme that people value social feedback that enhances their feelings of self-esteem/self-worth. Such feedback can be derived from material acquisitions, but the research reports that social sources are generally more important.

Lind and Tyler (1988) argue that people are interested in procedural fairness because being treated fairly reflects on their feelings of inclusion in a group as well as their perceived within-group status, both of which influence their identity and self-esteem.

This core idea, labeled the "group value" perspective, is developed and extended into the context of authority relations by the "relational model" of authority (Tyler & Lind, 1992) and into that of relationships within organizations by the "group engagement" model (Tyler & Blader, 2000). The "relational model" is an overview term that refers to this family of three models that were developed and tested over a period of approximately fifteen years, with each model building on and extending the insights of those that preceded it.

The common denominator associated with these models – and with all subsequent research inspired by them – is that people use the procedural justice they encounter in an interaction (or across interactions) as a cue for evaluating the nature of their relationship with the party enacting the procedure and the community that party represents. Fair procedures communicate a positive message regarding the nature of that relationship, while unfair procedures communicate the opposite message. These interactions can involve bilateral relationships, people's connections to authorities, and/or their relationship to organizations, communities, institutions, or societies. The importance of such relational messages, in turn, broadly explains the reactions that people have to the procedural justice they encounter. Studies show that people react more negatively to denial of respect than they do to denial of favorable material outcomes (Huo, 2002).

A relational argument is supported by research showing that people value fair procedures even when no outcome gains are available. This research finds that addressing an authority has value separate from the outcome of that encounter (Earley & Lind, 1987; Tyler, 1987). What matters is the belief that one's arguments have been taken seriously and considered. Second, elements of procedures that are least related to outcomes (respect, civility) are often the most impactful. Disrespect, discourtesy, and a failure to treat the individual with dignity frequently dominate people's concerns and grievances. Finally, the scope of procedural justice effects is defined by the groups with which a person identifies and whose judgments regarding that person have identity-relevant implications (Smith et al., 1998). Disrespect from outsiders has little to no impact on self-worth or self-esteem. Similarly, people who are alienated from institutions or who feel socially marginalized do not care about the status messages communicated by group authorities. A teenager in a gang may care little about messages that are communicated by a teacher but may define his or her self-worth and self-esteem in terms of the actions of others in the gang.

Why is being treated fairly or unfairly by police officers important to community residents? As community authorities, the police, like any representatives of society, convey messages to people regarding their inclusion and status in the community. When such authorities humiliate and demean people, they indicate that these people are marginal members of the community. When people bring a grievance to an authority, for example, they are acting on the belief that as members of society in good standing, they are entitled to highlight their issues and to have them taken seriously. Being listened to and viewing legal authorities as responsive to the needs and concerns thus expressed promotes feelings of status and inclusion (Murphy et al., 2022; Murphy & McCarthy, 2022).

Similar concerns arise when people are stopped by the police, and become even more prominent in this context because they feel vulnerable and often frightened. A comparable situation obtains when people call for help. Even if they never call the police, most people want to believe that if they needed help, the police would take their concerns seriously and try to help them. When minority communities consider themselves to be underserved, they often mean that their concerns and complaints are not taken seriously because their status in the community is low (Desmond-Harris, 2015; Gordon, 2022).

Similarly, most people in any community are not actively involved in criminal activity and feel devalued if they are treated as suspects, deviants, and potential criminals by the police. Even in high-crime neighborhoods, most people are not involved in criminal activity. Even people who are involved in crime want to receive decent and respectful treatment from the authorities who represent the community, and to be shown respect for their humanity even if their actions are condemned and they are punished.

Contact with the police can occur because people are stopped by the police or because they approach a police officer to obtain help. In both cases, research suggests that procedural justice is the strongest and most consistent factor shaping the ways in which people respond (Tyler & Huo, 2002). Consider the case of calls for help. The factor that most strongly influences satisfaction with the police is not speed of response or outcomes, but rather how fairly people feel they are treated by the responding officers.

Finally, it is important to highlight the fact that when people generalize from their personal experiences with the police to an overall view of police legitimacy, the key aspect of personal experience that affects this process is procedural justice. The actions of officers in specific encounters promote or undermine the legitimacy that people feel the police department has in their communities.

3.2 The Psychology of Authority

Taken together, these psychological views provide a model of authority that represents an alternative perspective to the instrumental view that has dominated much of the social science and policy literature. Like that view, legitimacy-based authority is a general model. Everyone is motivated to defer to authorities that they view as legitimate in the context of the groups to which they belong and with which they identify.

The advantage of a legitimacy-based model is that people defer to authority. This deference mitigates the costs of surveillance and sanctioning. The disadvantage of the legitimacy-based model is that it requires the development of legitimacy, a process that takes time and constrains authorities to pay attention to and be responsive to the issues that matter to their constituent communities.

3.2.1 Empirical Evaluations of the Legitimacy-Based Model

A key question pertains to whether there is evidence that legitimacy-based authority works. The idea of procedural justice has been the subject of considerable empirical research. Procedural justice findings have been replicated in a series of studies conducted by the Thibaut–Walker research group (see Lind & Tyler, 1988). These findings concerning procedural justice have been replicated by this group in a series of experimental studies. A strength of these studies is their high internal validity, while their weaknesses include the laboratory context and lack of measurement of perceived legitimacy as an outcome of personal experiences.

Following this initial work, the field of procedural justice rapidly became well established in the field of social psychology (Lind & Tyler, 1988). MacCoun (2005) conducted a review and found that the social psychological literature contained more than 700 articles pertaining to the topic of procedural justice. The review suggests that experimental variations in actual procedural justice and differences in perceived procedural justice across different settings are both consistently found to impact compliance and cooperation with authorities (MacCoun 2005). These effects were found using both experimental and correlational research designs. MacCoun (2005, p. 173) notes that "the sheer heterogeneity of tasks, domains, populations, designs, and analytic methods provides remarkable convergence and triangulation" in support of the core propositions of the model.

The theoretical elements highlighted by the psychological literature concerning procedural justice are also reviewed by Miller (2001), who identifies two behavioral consequences of procedural justice. The first is a marked inclination to comply with authorities; the second is an increased willingness to pursue group goals and concerns. Miller notes the absence of any negative consequences of emphasizing fair procedures. He further notes that such an emphasis valuably expands the universe of goals beyond the level of compliance to include actions that enhance the viability of organizations.

3.2.2 Procedural Justice in Management

As noted, much of the early research in this area did not focus on organizational settings. However, there is an area of social psychology that overlaps with the field of management, i.e., organizational behavior, an area that is concerned with authorities and institutions in work settings. The central arguments of procedural justice models were subsequently tested in management settings, and a distinct literature focusing on procedural justice emerged in the context of organizational psychology/organizational behavior.

Cohen-Charash and Spector (2001) review 190 studies (148 field studies and 42 laboratory studies) and find that variations in workplace characteristics reliably shape perceived procedural justice and thereby influence a variety of workplace behaviors. These variations particularly shape rule-following behavior.

Colquitt et al. (2001) review the justice literature and Colquitt et al. (2013) rereview both the original and the new literature and identify 493 distinct studies. In the larger rereview (Colquitt et al., 2013), these authors find significant overall influences of procedural justice on trust in management, organizational citizenship behavior (i.e., cooperation), task performance, and (negatively) counterproductive work behavior. The rereview finds equally strong relationships for studies that focus upon particular events as for those that make overall workplace evaluations.

In summary, the theoretical model underlying the procedural justice approach has been widely supported by studies that vary in terms of their focus and methodology. A striking point is the convergence of these findings. Many studies, including experimental variations in procedures, suggest that it is possible to reliably create policies and practices that influence perceived procedural justice. Studies also suggest that such variations shape not only perceived procedural justice but also compliance, cooperation, and a variety of other types of organizationally relevant behaviors. This finding echoes MacCoun's (2005) suggestion that variations in method or type of authority do not alter the basic conclusions reached.

3.3 Applying Theories from the Social Sciences

Considering the decidedly academic focus of early work in this area by Leventhal (1980) and Thibaut and Walker (1975), the impact of legitimacy-based models on policing is a striking illustration of the potential of psychological theories and research to have a strong impact on society. Anyone seeking to illustrate the famous quotation by Kurt Lewin that "there is nothing so practical as a good theory" (Hunt, 1987, p. 4) could highlight the way in which these ideas have permeated the policies and practices of legal institutions. Recent developments in this arena illustrate the value of theories in the social sciences for criminology and the development of policies in criminal law. The theoretical models and empirical studies pertaining to legitimacy and procedural justice–based policing policies have contributed to discussions regarding twenty-first-century American policing.

The background to this work draws on the field of psychology. It is reasonable to ask why psychologists are drawn to addressing issues in the criminal legal system. In the case of legitimacy-based policing, the answer to this question is that we have been asked to do so by policing scholars and criminal legal authorities.

In the case of one of the authors of this Element (Tyler), my early work involved research in conflict management. It drew on psychological theories and tested them in both laboratory and field settings. It was not, however, targeted at criminal legal authorities. When I was a researcher at the American Bar Foundation, I was invited by the courts to address a concern expressed by judges: resistance to compliance with judicial orders. This concern led me to study litigants and, in conjunction with the evolving mediation and alternative dispute resolution (ADR) movements and various forms of work that included collaboration with researchers at the Institute of Civil Justice of the RAND corporation, to consider the type of forums that led to dispute resolutions that were acceptable to the parties involved in civil cases.

More recently, I have been drawn into discussions on policing and police reform. I was first asked to provide evidence to the 2004 National Academy of Sciences committee on policing (Skogan & Frydl, 2004). This report articulated legitimacy as an important goal of policing, and my involvement was the beginning of a series of efforts culminating in the Task Force on 21st Century Policing instituted in 2015 by President Obama. The 2004 report suggested that legitimacy should be a concern in policing, while the 2015 Task Force identified legitimacy as the first principle of policing and suggested a focus on strategies to obtain and maintain public trust.

Less publicly visible but equally important was a parallel set of efforts in the policy arena. The Community Oriented Policing Services office (COPS), under the direction of Bernard Melekian as well as Ellen Scrivner and Laurie Robinson at the National Institute of Justice, hosted a series of meetings with police leaders to promote these ideas and integrate them into COPS activities. The Department of Justice, under Eric Holder and Karol Mason, funded a national pilot program in six cities to evaluate and suggest improvements in policing policies and practices. The Chicago Police Department, under the leadership of superintendent Garry McCarthy, developed a procedural justice training program through its police academy. All these efforts helped introduce a set of academic ideas into the arena of policing.

The 2015 establishment of a Task Force by Obama marked a high point of momentum for national police reform. That momentum declined at the federal level with the election of President Trump and recent efforts to revive it at the federal level have led to executive but not legislative actions. Locally, a variety of efforts have been made at community and state levels. Some national policing groups, in particular the International Association of Chiefs of Police, have continued to advocate for police attention to issues of public trust and confidence.

The effort to collect complete and accurate data about policing has been intertwined with these theoretical advances and has been Caroline Nobo's focus as a national expert on criminal justice data and infrastructure. Her concern has been on translating data into policy. Efforts to develop evidence-informed policies for policing depend upon having data available for analysis, so articulating theory-based ideas and gathering appropriate data to test those models are both central to the work outlined in this Element.

Our focus is on strategies for the implementation of these new ideas in the context of policing.

4 Legitimacy-Based Policing

The legitimacy-based policing model is a straightforward application of the general legitimacy-based model that we have outlined (Section 3) to issues in policing. The strategies and tactics used by the police determine whether those they encounter and people in the community more generally evaluate them as acting in procedurally just ways. This evaluation in turn determines whether they are considered to be legitimate. In the case of the police, this legitimacy primarily pertains to whether people defer to police directives. However, a further goal is to guarantee that the police generally promote law-abiding behavior in people's everyday lives, even when they are not interacting directly with a police officer.

As mentioned, police forces across the United States decided to pursue the goal of focusing on police legitimacy. Although this decision was a reaction to low levels of public trust, it is clear that a legitimacy-based model would not be able to attain general acceptance if it were not also able to motivate compliance, since compliance has been a key metric for police success.

So does legitimacy motivate compliance? This issue is addressed by Tyler (2006b) in a longitudinal survey. His results, drawn from interviews with a sample of Chicago residents, support the argument that legitimacy shapes compliance. A direct comparison with the influence of the perceived risk of being caught and sanctioned suggests that perceived legitimacy is as influential as concerns regarding sanctioning. If the only goal is crime suppression via compliance, either model represents an approach that can be viable. This finding is important because when the public react to policies pertaining to the police, they consider the implications of changes in policing for crime and public safety (Vaughn, Peyton, & Huber, 2022). And it suggests that a focus on legitimacy would not undermine public safety.

Since this early work, a number of studies have demonstrated that greater legitimacy increases compliance in the context of personal interactions, particularly during stops by the police. For example, Tyler and Huo (2002) report the results of a study concerning compliance during personal encounters with the police. One influence on compliance is whether the police act in a procedurally just manner during the encounter.[5] Compliance is also related to people's views regarding the general legitimacy of the police.[6] The key point is that overall legitimacy distinctly influences compliance, controlling for the events that occur during the experience.

Legitimacy also shapes compliance by impacting everyday compliance with the law. Sunshine and Tyler (2003) report the results of two cross-sectional surveys of New Yorkers. Tyler and Fagan (2008) focus on data collected from a different panel of New Yorkers. And Tyler and Jackson (2014) report the results of a 2012 national cross-sectional survey of Americans. These studies consistently indicate that legitimacy is linked to compliance. They share the common feature of being nonexperimental, so an important advance in recent years is the fact that experimental studies have contributed to the policing literature in support of compliance.

A recent meta-analysis examines the literature concerning the police and evaluates the impact of legitimacy on compliance (Walters & Bolger, 2018). These authors' overall review of studies reveals 196 effect sizes from 95 samples that examined the influence of procedural justice and/or legitimacy on compliance. In the case of legitimacy, the results from cross-sectional studies suggest that legitimacy does influence compliance. The authors conclude that "legitimacy beliefs are instrumental in promoting compliance with the law" (Walters & Bolger, 2018, p. 341). Their review supports the argument that legitimacy-based policing is as effective in securing immediate compliance as other contemporary approaches. This conclusion is further supported by recent

---

[5] Compliance is related to the nature of the events that occur during the encounter, including neutrality (beta = 0.31, $p < 0.001$) and interpersonal respect (beta = 0.42, $p < 0.001$).

[6] (beta = 0.13, $p < 0.001$).

studies of the impact of legitimacy on people's willingness to follow COVID-19 restrictions (Folmer et al., 2021; Kooistra et al., 2021; Murphy et al., 2020; Reinders et al., 2020; Van Rooij et al., 2021).

While studies pertaining to the legitimacy–compliance relationship are largely correlational, experimental evidence is also reported. Dickson, Gordon, & Huber (2022) use an experimental approach to demonstrate that legitimacy shapes compliance behavior in an enforcement context. In their study, these authors "exogenously manipulate perceptions of legitimacy holding fixed the material incentives created" (Dickson, Gordon, & Huber, 2022, p. 9) and find an impact on citizen behavior.

Legitimacy also shapes cooperation. In this case, Bolger and Walters (2019) highlight 200 effect sizes from 88 samples. Their results indicate that legitimacy directly influences cooperation. The conclusions of these reviews are supported both by studies that employ subjective measures to assess willingness to cooperate (see Mazerolle et al., 2012; Wolfe et al., 2016) and by studies using objective measures of citizen cooperation (Dai, Frank, & Sun, 2011; Mastrofski, Snipes, & Supina, 1996; Mazerolle et al., 2013b).

An example of cooperation is calling the police for help. Desmond, Papachristos, and Kirk (2016) tested the argument that police legitimacy determines whether people decide to call the police. These authors show that perceived illegitimacy leads to a decline in residents' tendency to call the police for help. So whether the police are viewed as legitimate is central to whether people proactively contact the police.

In sum, these studies demonstrate that legitimacy shapes both compliance and cooperation. Recent research (Goff, Swencionis, & Tyler, 2022) shows in further detail that when the police are viewed as legitimate, they are perceived as better able to manage crime. Strikingly, if the police are viewed as more legitimate, people rate their ability to manage crime as greater when either coercive or noncoercive approaches are used. Legitimate police are granted discretion regarding how to pursue the goal of crime control.

4.1 Procedural Justice

The second key empirical question pertains to whether procedural justice matters in shaping legitimacy. The central conclusion of the procedural justice literature is that when people encounter authorities, their evaluations of the perceived fairness of the procedures through which authority is exercised influence legitimacy more strongly than does the perceived outcome of the encounter (Tyler, 2006b; Tyler & Jackson, 2014; Tyler, Fagan, & Geller, 2014). Donner et al. (2015) review twenty-eight studies of the police and conclude that procedural justice activities in the context of police interactions with the public positively influence public views of police legitimacy and trust in the police.

Similarly, when people make overall assessments of the legitimacy of a criminal justice institution in their community, they focus on the ways in which members of that institution generally deal with the public (Sunshine & Tyler, 2003; Tyler, 2006b; Tyler & Jackson, 2014; Tyler, Fagan, & Geller, 2014).

Tyler and Jackson (2014) draw on the results of a survey to examine the role played by procedural justice in shaping legitimacy at two levels. At the personal level, these authors consider the impacts of outcome favorability, outcome lawfulness, and procedural justice on overall police legitimacy. The results of a regression indicate that procedural justice is most noteworthy (beta = 0.51, p < 0.001), followed by outcome lawfulness (beta = 0.10, p < 0.05), and outcome favorability (beta = 0.02, n.s.). These judgments explain 37 percent of the variance in overall police legitimacy. At the community level, the authors compare police effectiveness, police lawfulness, and general police procedural justice. The results of a regression indicate that procedural justice is most noteworthy (beta = 0.42, p < 0.001), followed by outcome lawfulness (beta = 0.33, p < 0.001). and outcome favorability (beta = 0.19, p < 0.001). Overall, 64 percent of the variance in legitimacy is thus explained.

There is also an emerging body of experimental studies investigating the impact of procedurally just treatment on citizen attitudes toward the police. These studies examine whether manipulations in the procedural justice of treatment by the police influence perceptions of police legitimacy and cooperation with the police. Mazerolle et al. (2013a) use an experimental design to examine police stops in Australia and find that a single experience of heightened procedural justice generalizes to an influence on trust in the police in the community.

In the case of assessing the impact of procedural fairness during police contact on subsequent willingness to cooperate with the police, Mazerolle et al. (2013b) create a combined measure of self-reported behavior summarizing ongoing compliance and future willingness to cooperate. These authors evaluate five experimental studies that provide eight outcome measures. They conclude that the results suggest that the "interventions had [a] large, significant, positive association with a combined measure of compliance and cooperation" (Mazerolle et al., 2013b, p. 261).

Mazerolle et al. (2014, p. 28) report the results of an extended meta-analysis of procedural justice effects. In reviewing community policing efforts that contain procedural justice elements, the authors find four studies that explore the influence of these elements on compliance/cooperation and report three significant relationships in the expected direction. With respect to restorative justice conferencing, they find four studies that examine the influence of this factor on compliance/cooperation and four significant relationships (Mazerolle et al., 2014, p. 29). The authors conclude that procedural justice has positive effects on perceived legitimacy and that these effects jointly shape self-reported compliance/cooperation.

Flippin, Reisig, and Trinkner (2019) add experimental support to these conclusions. These authors report the results of a vignette-based study using a factorial design. In that study, university students read a vignette concerning a particular emergency (burglary, traffic accident) in which a call had been made to 911. The vignettes varied in terms of the procedural injustice exhibited by the police and the seriousness of the emergency. Students who read about a scenario in which the police were procedurally unjust indicated a lower likelihood of calling 911 in a future situation and expressed less willingness to cooperate with the police after their arrival in such a situation. The seriousness of the incident in terms of monetary losses was less significant than prior injustice. A recent review of experimental studies supports the core argument that variations in procedural justice influence police legitimacy (Nivette, Nagel, & Stan, 2022).

Most recently, Weisburd et al. (2022) report the results of a field experiment involving procedural justice training as part of a study of hot-spot policing (the strategy of concentrating police in high-crime areas). These authors note that procedural-justice trained police officers made fewer arrests and were less likely to be viewed by respondents as harassing citizens or using unnecessary force. In addition, there was a 14 percent decline in the rate of crime. The decrease in perceptions of the unnecessary use of force may be due to the finding that officers who are focused on procedural justice are less likely to employ force (Piza & Sytsma, 2022; Wood, Tyler, & Papachristos, 2020)

This review of the literature is not intended to constitute a complete review of research in this field. The number of relevant studies is already so large that meta-analyses are being conducted. In particular, there is a robust stream of literature focused on procedural justice in societies worldwide. The goal here is to highlight the empirical literature in support of the argument that legitimacy-based policing is not merely a theoretical proposition but also has empirical support.

One of the challenges associated with the police is distinguishing between the influence of perceived procedural justice and that of other possible antecedents of police behavior. As an example, Nägel and Vera (2021) report the results of a cross-societal study of trust in the police, finding that corruption is a key antecedent of trust. Is corruption a performance issue, a distributive justice issue, or a procedural justice issue? It is easy to see how corruption can be viewed as an unfair procedure (i.e., featuring a lack of neutrality and a denial of voice or serving as an example of untrustworthy motives). In such situations, it is difficult to determine whether the empirical findings support or do not support a procedural justice perspective because it involves the police behaving in ways that are not directly identified as procedural justice but that contain the same concepts as procedural justice.

Another example of this difficulty is the effort to distinguish between procedural justice effects and the influence of sanctions. It has already been noted that sanctions shape behavior. Yasrebi-De Kom et al. (2022), however, find that the impact of sanctions interacts with procedural justice. More severe sanctions influence deterrence, but only if they are paired with procedural justice. This impact is a moderation effect.

There is also a mediation issue associated with sanctions research. Studies concerning the effects of sanctions do not typically measure intervening psychological judgments. Rather, researchers assume that if sanctions shape behavior, they do so by increasing the fear of punishment, and so researchers do not tend to measure risk assessments. They assume they are the mediating variable. Under these conditions, it is difficult to determine whether sanction effects are solely the result of higher risk assessments and not of other factors such as procedural justice. Correlational studies, for example, suggest that a system that includes sanctions is viewed as more procedurally just if, as noted above, these sanctions are enacted fairly.

4.2 Breadth of the Model

The original development of the legitimacy-based policing model took place in an American context. In addition, as is clear, many of the comments made in the discussion of this model pertain particularly to the American style of policing. This specificity makes sense given that trust in the police is considerably higher in other Western democracies. For example, 74 percent of the residents of England, 77 percent of those of New Zealand and 68 percent of those in Australia express trust in the police. In Germany, the figure is 79 percent, and in the Netherlands, it is 77 percent (Nägel & Vera, 2021). The question is whether the lower levels found in the United States are linked to experiences of policing as being more unjust in America.

It is natural to inquire into how broadly this model can be extended across societies. A complete review of international research is beyond the scope of this Element (see Jackson, 2018). However, important support for the model has been found in research in the United Kingdom (Jackson et al., 2012) and across the European Union (Hough, Jackson, & Bradford, 2013).

It is important to note that the model is not always supported. As an example, Tankebe (2009) reports that public views of the police in Ghana are strongly instrumental in character. This study highlights the fact that when the police are viewed as corrupt (i.e., unjust in terms of their decision-making procedures), people shift to an instrumental evaluation of the police. It is unrealistic to expect procedural justice to have an impact if the procedures used are fundamentally unjust. Early experimental evidence by psychologists shows that when people have evidence that a procedure is unfair, they react to their experiences in accordance with the favorability of their outcomes (Lind & Lissak, 1985).

4.3 Ethnicity and Policing

Our discussion in this Element began by suggesting that policing issues are not merely issues of racial injustice. The warrior type of policing harms everyone. On the other hand, it is also important to recognize that it does not harm everyone to the same degree. It is particularly important to examine whether the effects of procedural justice can be found among the most heavily impacted subgroup of the population, which, in America, is the Black community.

A key point that arises from an emerging stream of literature pertaining to heavily impacted subgroups is that procedural justice enhances legitimacy among the members of all racial groups. This argument is made by Tyler and Huo (2002) and has been called the invariance argument. It has subsequently been supported in whole or in part by a series of studies (Aiello, 2021; Brown & Reisig, 2019; Pina-Sánchez & Brunton-Smith, 2020; Reisig et al., 2021; Wheelock, Stroshine, & O'Hear, 2019; Wolfe et al., 2016; Zahnow, Mazerolle, & Pang, 2021).

There are clear limits to an invariance model. As noted in our discussion of theoretical models in Section 3, concerns regarding procedural justice are linked to perceived group membership. Outsiders are less impacted by the actions of within-group authorities. Consequently, people who are alienated from their society and its institutions may not be affected by procedural justice. Two examples are a study of minorities in Australia (Sargeant, Davoren, & Murphy, 2021) and an investigation of homeless individuals in London (Kyprianides et al., 2021).

Another pattern of behavior exhibited by marginalized groups is to focus on the procedural justice associated with specific officers and to react behaviorally to that factor without developing a view of the legitimacy of the police as a whole. In other words, authority relationships may be more personalized. The pattern found among Muslims living in London is to respond to the procedural justice of particular officers by deferring to those specific authorities, without any intervention by an overriding idea of legitimacy (Huq, Tyler, & Schulhofer, 2011).

4.4 Implications for Policing

4.4.1 Dealing with the Public

From a legal perspective, the US Constitution does not mandate any particular form or style of policing or any type of treatment that people are entitled to receive from the police. The law focuses on the conditions under which a police officer is entitled to stop, question, search, detain, and/or arrest a member of the community. Police officers are trained to recognize the circumstances under which they can intervene in people's lives. If a police officer has legal grounds to stop someone, there are no Constitutional standards indicating that they must listen to that person, explain their actions, and/or treat the person with courtesy or respect. Similarly, the capacity to deploy force means that officers can typically compel obedience, as least within specific contexts. The limits placed on the police are primarily linked to the illegality of using unreasonable force or acting based on bias.

This analysis indicates some of the reasons why police officers may benefit from focusing on the ways in which they treat people during encounters, even if such a focus is not legally required and may not be necessary to ensure immediate compliance with police orders. Achieving the benefits of the advocated modifications in policing can be facilitated by a change in police culture.

With respect to the type of contact, adopting this approach also highlights the advantages of shifting police culture from a proactive model focused on preventing crime via investigatory contact to a model in which the police focus on providing services and addressing requests for assistance.

Proactive stops, especially investigatory stops, have been noted to contribute to distrust (Epp, Maynard-Moody, & Haidt-Markel, 2014). From the perspective of this Element, service tasks represent an opportunity to inspire public support for the police.

Service delivery is viewed differently from the perspective of a procedural justice model. A minor crime may be likely to remain unsolved, and such crimes can be addressed via a form that can be completed by mail or over the Internet. What would a police department gain from dispatching officers to the scene in such a case or at least having a personal conversation with a person who calls instead of simply providing him or her with a form? The police would gain an opportunity to develop legitimacy.

This situation is only one example of a wide variety of activities that the police might perform to develop trust. Peyton and colleagues (2019), for example, told officers to travel to people's homes and ask them about problems in their neighborhoods. Also, police officers work with summer camps and may cooperate with people to resolve everyday problems such as garbage collection or connecting with social services.

In terms of training, focusing on the interactional dynamics of contact with the public and increasing a department's service orientation both suggest the desirability of retraining officers with the goal of shifting from a warrior to a service orientation. Quattlebaum and Tyler (2020) emphasize the mismatch between what officers do and the ways in which they have been trained and equipped. The warrior skill set is not only unhelpful for dealing more effectively with many everyday issues faced by the police; it actually intensifies conflict in many cases by characterizing every situation as pertaining to control and domination, thereby provoking hostility and anger. The presence of weapons, especially when coupled with verbal and nonverbal displays of dominance and control, defines every situation as potentially rife with conflict and highlights vulnerability, thus amplifying civilians' fear. This claim is especially true for minority group members who often have a history of individual and collective mistrust of the police.

The problems associated with the warrior style in the context of American policing have been intensified by social forces that have nothing to do with the police. In recent decades, American governments have continually retreated from the task of providing social services to urban communities. As a result, the police have increasingly been required to provide a wide variety of services, ranging from managing everyday disorder and domestic disputes to dealing with homelessness and mental illness, for which an armed police officer who is trained to deploy force to coerce compliance is not a desirable solution.

Many police officers agree with this claim and do not consider these tasks to be "real" police work. They have been drawn into performing them due to the lack of other municipal services. The police are increasingly the default agency for dealing with a range of social issues and urban problems for which officers are not trained, in which they have little interest, and at which they are not particularly adept.

A solution to this problem is to change the culture of police departments and the style of policing. A warrior style is not intrinsic to policing and, in fact, this style has not been used by the police throughout American history. It became more dominant during an earlier era of high crime, as we have outlined. As this review suggests, an alternative model has been proven to be as effective in suppressing crime and to potentially be able to create a broader framework within which policing can be valuable.

Quattlebaum and Tyler (2020) suggest a variety of ways of reorganizing departments so that they can better achieve the goal of making the police relevant to the community. If it is possible to retrain officers to be more focused on procedural justice, then one approach is to employ a model based on changing the culture of the police so that officers have broader skill sets. To the extent that it is not possible to retrain current police officers, another approach is to lower the number of traditionally trained and equipped police and restrict them to a crime fighting role, thereby freeing up resources to allow social services tasks to be performed by officers specializing in service roles or by social workers outside the department. Bringing people with diverse skills into the police department, either as a new form of police officer or as embedded civilians, is one possibility for change.

In accordance with the examples of traffic control or auxiliary officers, it is possible to imagine unarmed and unsworn officers playing a variety of roles for which they are better trained, because they do not take on the traditional roles and obligations associated with armed officers.

The point is that there are a variety of ways in which departments can be restructured to better meet the goal of effective policing. Does this imply that more fundamental critiques of the police, such as the movement to eliminate police departments altogether (i.e., to "defund the police") are erroroneous? It is important to recognize that reducing police funding is only one of a variety of possible approaches, and to evaluate this approach in comparison to alternatives. Redefining the goals and tactics of policing is an alternative to defunding the police.

To consider the best ways of reorganizing police services, several questions must be addressed. The first pertains to whether repurposing traditional police is the best way of addressing community problems. Traditionally, police are trained and equipped to manage problems that require the use of force, which is a small subset of the problems they actually encounter. Retraining makes them more effective in a broader role and appears to be an obvious reform.

Why would retraining be a problem? Consider the case of firefighters. In America, the number of fires is strikingly low and continually declining. Simultaneously, the number of firefighters is increasing. How is this mismatch justified (Stromberg, 2015)? One possible justification is that many departments repurpose firefighters to provide Emergency Medical Services (EMT) training, which is why fire trucks frequently respond to medical emergencies. This repurposing is an adaptation, but is it a beneficial one? It costs more for firefighters to respond to a medical emergency with a fire truck, which means that there are fewer ambulances and fewer EMTs available to respond. However, this shift also gives existing firefighters the capacity to deal with a broader range of problems. The point is that repurposing existing staff is not always or self-evidently the best way of addressing an issue. It may also make sense to downsize and reinvest in a different institutional model. However, repurposing is a politically attractive approach that builds upon existing institutions.

One example of a field that has benefited from role differentiation is that of medicine. Doctors used to ride in ambulances, but today they do not. Instead, EMTs arrive on the scene and coordinate with doctors to bring people to hospitals. The risk–benefit balance is that while some people may die at the scene because there is no doctor in the ambulance, more people, overall, can be saved by having more ambulances available due to the cost savings resulting from not requiring doctors to ride in ambulances.

Triage entails differentiation. Retraining an armed officer who is responsible for and trained in the deployment of force to engage in procedural justice, de-escalation, and conflict management may be better than traditional policing, but it may not be the optimal solution. It might be better to differentiate these tasks and have a small group of armed officers who are trained in the use of force and a large set of social workers. The key is a triage-based approach focused on the necessary skills and the best way of allocating them. One focus of reform in this case is the people who dispatch services.

In the context of the current policing model, there seems to be a considerable amount of low-hanging fruit in terms of staff differentiation. A great deal of what officers do on an everyday basis does not call for the capabilities of a highly trained officer who is able to use force in situations that seldom require it. Repeated studies demonstrate that it would be possible to save a substantial amount of money by deploying armed officers more effectively by requiring them to respond only, or primarily, to situations that benefit from their skill set. As in the case of medicine, making such a judgment requires us to accept that situations will always emerge in which it would be helpful to have an armed officer at the scene. Calling for backup is not always the optimal solution. The system-level argument is that the money saved by differentiation can be reallo-cated to other tasks, which can lower the crime rate and reduce the overall risk to both unarmed and armed officers. Of course, unarmed officers lower the risk of injury to all parties to the extent that armed police encourage conflict spirals.

Making an argument of this type requires us to consider the consequences of the presence of unarmed officers in a gun-obsessed society such as the United States. Although the conventional wisdom that being armed makes officers safer is nearly an unassailable aspect of police thinking, empirical studies do not support this claim. It must first be recognized that there are many challenges associated with the task of addressing this question empirically. However, as one example, Farmer and Evans (2020) compare similar communities that vary in terms of the degree to which the police are armed and these authors do not find that unarmed officers are at greater risk of death on the job. They conclude that "what we can state as a clear and repeated finding is the absence of definitive evidence to support the contention that routinely arming police officers inevitably and invariably increases community or police safety" (Evans & Farmer, 2021, p. 99).

Similarly, Mummolo (2018) does not find that increasing the militarization of police officers enhances their safety. The police may believe that possessing an armored car makes them safer, but that belief does not have empirical support.

One reason for the fact that being armed may not be linked to officer safety is that people in the community seldom initiate actions against police officers. The police are more likely to use force to compel obedience than to defend themselves. In everyday policing, most people do not resist police officers, and their actions involve nonresponsiveness or efforts to flee. Stoughton suggests that "the vast majority of the time, ... officers use force aggressively, not defensively ... [T]hey act forcefully to establish control over a suspect rather than to defend themselves, a third party, or the suspect from some imminent harm" (Stoughton, 2014, p. 868). Consequently, injury to the officer is unlikely unless the officers precipitate the actions that lead to such a situation.

What is necessary is systematic research concerning the circumstances in which being armed is beneficial. To the degree that it is not beneficial, the possibility of differentiating police responses gains credence, as does the possibility of creating a larger pool of differently trained and equipped officers.

4.4.2 Diversion

A further implication of the service model is that police benefit from emphasizing diversion from the criminal legal system toward various forms of community treatment. Negative police contact is particularly associated with discretionary police interventions in people's lives, and such contact is frequently associated with carceral outcomes such as arrest. It is important to note that the police have alternatives to arresting people. They can admonish them informally in a variety of ways (Muir, 1979) and thereby create possibilities to develop trust. They can also help people solve their problems (Beckett, 2016). An example of this approach is the Seattle LEAD program, in which officers take people to treatment centers rather than making arrests (Clifasefi, Lonczak, & Collins, 2017).

4.4.3 Police Tactics

Another type of change involves greater use of de-escalatory tactics. Although rushing into danger may be necessary in a few situations, in many cases securing the situation and waiting for backup is an equally desirable or even superior response. This approach is relevant because if officers on the scene are unarmed, securing the scene and waiting for armed backup makes the necessity of every officer being armed less pressing. Since being trained and authorized to use force requires extra and ongoing expenses from a department, the implementation of a small unit that can be rapidly deployed (such as a special weapons and tactics [SWAT] team) would lead to substantial cost savings.

4.5 Internal Procedural Justice

The early application of procedural justice to policing was focused on police relations with people in the community. However, it was soon recognized that police officers themselves frequently feel that procedural injustice is an issue in their departments. This has led the police to consider the application of procedural justice to internal police department dynamics (Trinkner, Tyler, & Goff, 2016). The management literature is relevant to this situation. The argument is that officers are less likely to adopt a procedural justice approach in the community if they do not experience such an approach in their own work organizations.

The management literature focuses on the procedures that managers use when dealing with their employees. Research shows that the principles of procedural justice apply to both private and public organizations, including the police, the courts, and prisons. This research has led to the recognition that one way in which police departments can promote broader goals is to reorganize themselves internally based on the principles of procedural justice. A number of studies in this context support the benefits of this model. Officers need to feel that their superiors treat them in procedurally fair ways. When officers believe that the authorities in their own department are fair, a number of positive consequences ensue: They exhibit more job satisfaction and higher levels of engagement in their jobs; they are more committed to their work; they report lower levels of stress and therefore experience fewer mental and physical health issues; and they report adopting a style of policing more focused on fairness when dealing with people in the community (see Weisburd & Majmundar, 2018 for a review of this evidence).

This situation illustrates the benefits of procedural justice for the police themselves. Procedural fairness in a department leads to less stress for police officers: It is important to recognize that policing is stressful and that methods must be developed to facilitate officer wellness. One example of such a benefit for officers is legitimacy-based policing, which makes police jobs less physically stressful and psychologically challenging. The everyday experience of encountering a distrustful or even hostile public and dealing with frequent pushback against their authority makes policing a job that is associated with high rates of physical and mental health problems. Long-term stress exacerbates many heart-related illnesses, and police officers have one of the poorest cardio-vascular disease health profiles of any occupation (Hartley et al., 2011). Similarly, rates of alcoholism and suicide among officers are high (Mumford, Liu, & Taylor, 2021). Violanti et al. (2013) report that on average, police officers have "significantly lower" life expectancies than the population in general. For example, a 50-year-old officer is expected to live an 7.8 additional years beyond the age of 50, compared to an average of 35 years for the general population.

This last point also highlights the fact that there are several ways of promoting procedural justice in the community. The internal procedural justice approach has the advantage of not being prescriptive. Officers do not need to be ordered to be fair to people in the community. They recognize the value of taking such an approach because they experience procedural justice in their work environment. It becomes their accustomed style of interaction. The literature concerning internal procedural justice highlights the multiple groups that benefit from a climate of procedural justice. Supervisors obtain the benefit of a more amenable workforce. Officers have a better job experience. The public feel that they are treated more fairly. This environment is the type of win–win situation that typically promotes successful institutional change.

4.6 Methodology

The introduction of procedural justice to the field of policing has also highlighted issues pertaining to methodology. Psychology is the ultimate experimental science, and much of the early evidence regarding procedural justice is provided by experiments (randomized control trials or RCTs). However, that evidence has been critiqued by legal scholars due to its lack of external validity since a great deal of it reflects findings regarding artificial experiments, often using student subjects, and can involve simulations, scenarios, and vignettes. Although the studies by Thibaut and Walker (1975) focus on law, their work has been criticized for its use of laboratory methods: simulated disputes, student participants, and the use of law school students as legal authorities.

Much of our work in this context has taken place in field settings; survey research has been conducted to collect data, and correlation-based regression techniques have been used to analyze the findings. Why was our research conducted in this way? One reason is that this work represents a reaction to critiques of the laboratory focus exhibited by social psychology. To counteract these concerns, our studies utilize real-world experiences with the police and the courts. Recognizing the problems of causal inference associated with such studies, panel designs have been used, and participants have been interviewed multiple times.

The ideal way to respond to critiques of laboratory experiences is by conducting field experiments (i.e., RCTs). These experiments are conducted in real-world settings and involve actual policy variations by legal authorities by reference to real-world communities. However, field experiments require the cooperation of existing authorities. Our personal experience has been that authorities are often unwilling to test ideas that they have decided are not valuable based upon their previously existing views. To give one specific example, our panel studies of the experiences of New Yorkers with the practices of the New York Police Department were funded by the federal government. One reason for addressing the study of stop, question, and frisk tactics using surveys was that the local government could not prevent this type of research from being conducted but could decline to enact RCT trials of new policing practices.

Relying on RCT studies gives existing authorities veto power over the ability to test new ideas. This situation raises important questions concerning the relationship between scholarship and existing authorities. Who defines the research agenda? One view is that the role of researchers is to test the value of policies and practices that the authorities have decided they might implement. A recent example is the use of body cameras. These cameras have been widely adopted without substantial evidence that they are effective. However, a growing body of research focuses on evaluating them. The problem with this approach is that there is not a great deal of opportunity for scholars to promote new models of policing. Until recently, legitimacy-based policing was one such example.

One of the most important developments associated with increased attention to the ideas of legitimacy and perceived procedural justice is that criminologists have focused their high levels of research expertise on testing these ideas in the context of policing. These field tests employ a variety of methods, including randomized field trials, and they have widely, although not universally, supported the tenets of the model.

Consider several recent studies as illustrations. Canales (2022a) randomly assigned 1,854 police officers in Mexico City to create an evaluation of procedural justice training. This study is noteworthy due to its several methodological innovations. Officer conceptions of their job were collected by asking them to take pictures of aspects of their day that they felt reflected their job. Officers then participated in in-depth interviews to examine the narratives they associated with those pictures. The impact of behavior in the community was assessed by a "mystery shopper" study in which officers responded to a call for an everyday disorder complaint. In reality, the officers were interacting with professional actors enacting a standardized script. The authors coded videotapes of officer behavior regarding the management of these everyday disorder complaints. Their evaluations demonstrate that trained officers conceptualize their job differently and interact in different ways with citizens.

Weisburd et al. (2022) conducted a randomized trial of policing in 120 crime hotspots across 3 cities. The treatment used was training in procedurally just policing. The authors report that the treated group interacted with citizens in more procedurally just ways and made fewer arrests. An evaluation of these changes found that people in these hotspots were less likely to view the police as harassing citizens or using unnecessary force. There was also a significant decline in criminal incidents in treated areas.

4.7 Implementing Change

Is change possible? This question highlights an issue of organizational change. Unlike private companies, which face market pressures, the police are more insulated from many pressures for change. While crime rates have decreased sharply since the 1980s, police departments have not correspondingly decreased in size, attesting to their capacity to resist change even in the face of evidence that policing levels are unconnected to the ability to manage crime (Bjerk, 2022; Bouie, 2022; Bump, 2020).

Studies of police departments suggest several important factors that determine whether change occurs. One such factor is external pressure. Sustained pressure from the public or organized groups such as Black Lives Matter, community churches, or business organizations has been found to be fundamental to organizational change (Canales, 2022b, 2022c). This pressure can arise from instances of perceived police misconduct or from the high costs associated with everyday policing, including the impact of paying for civil claims against the police. Such pressure must be long-term and transcend momentary crime "panics" pertaining to high visibility crimes, which often encourage a default response based on a return to carceral logic, even when the crimes in question communicate very little information regarding everyday risks in a community.

Highlighting the need for sustained pressure suggests that one key issue in reform is the question of who the target of such pressure should be. A traditional target is the police chief, a figure who is visible and who can be viewed as reasonably accountable. However, chiefs typically conform their actions to pressure from mayors and city councils, so it is important to identify pressure points in the political system. One such pressure point is the cost of police departments, both in terms of paying highly skilled but expensive armed officers and in terms of the collateral costs of civil case settlements resulting from police actions. As crime rates decline and municipal budgets face more stress, the possibility of pressuring political leaders becomes more feasible. On the other hand, recent events make it clear that leaders must constantly balance support for reform with public fears regarding safety, fears that are often only loosely linked to actual risk and highly responsive to sensational events.

A key to change is altering the internal dynamics within a department. Often, procedural justice training is simply added to an existing department. Such training frequently has, at best, a minor impact. Change must involve obtaining buy-in from mid-level supervisors, who are central to field officers' understanding of their job. Studies find that relationships with these immediate superiors have the greatest impact on the ways in which everyday policing is enacted by officers (Geller & Toch, 1959). In the American policing system, police chiefs come and go, but middle managers remain, so they are key to sustained change.

Along with buy-in from supervisors, it is important to change rules regarding what is valued and recognized as exemplary officer achievement as well as the ways in which decisions are made regarding pay and promotion. Who is the officer of the month and why is this person being honored? How is the path to advancement defined? A service culture defines these metrics differently than a warrior culture. If a department glorifies its warriors, other officers tend to desire to emulate the warrior culture.

Finally, metrics must be diversified. One reason that the police focus on crime rates is that crime rate statistics are collected and are available as an index of success. It is important to supplement such statistics with measures of public trust. This task can be accomplished through exit interviews with people who come into contact with the police, via community surveys, or in both ways.

5 Expanding the Goals of Policing

This section outlines an additional advantage of adopting the legitimacy-based policing model: Namely, adopting this model creates an opportunity for the police to pursue a broader set of goals than crime management. The primary goal that is effectively addressed by a sanctions-based model is crime suppression. As noted, irrespective of whether this model is the best at suppressing crime, sanctions-based deterrence does significantly influence the rate of crime. However, this model is not very effective at pursuing a broader set of goals that the police might want to pursue. We have already outlined the possibility of managing crime using a model that relies more heavily on voluntary deference and obtaining willing cooperation. In this section, we suggest a further expansion of the goals of policing to the context of community development. Our suggestion is that the framework of legitimacy-based policing makes this extension possible.

If the legitimacy-based approach to crime management gains traction in policing, does this advance address the problems that arise in communities? Over recent decades, discussions concerning legitimacy have typically accepted the definition of the goal of policing identified by the coercive model. The goal has remained harm reduction via crime control, but a different set of police strategies for achieving this goal have been advocated. The assumption has also remained that the key agency necessary to achieve this goal is the police. Policy changes focus on combatting policing excesses, such as the unnecessary use of force. In this section, we continue to focus on a police perspective but suggest that the police can aid community development.

One of the limitations of the police's focus on crime suppression is that it has not been directed at the root causes of crime. Police do not have a long-term strategy for decreasing the need for policing by improving the economic, social, and political vitality of communities. As noted, the deterrence model is based on the premise that a police presence will always be necessary to suppress crime, which will always be a problem in the community. An alternative approach would be to seek to change communities so that less crime occurs. Can the police help achieve that goal? Even during the era of carceral logic, some police leaders have recognized that you cannot arrest your way out of crime. If legitimacy promotes community development, resident engagement, and long-term community vitality, this suggests a way of diminishing the necessity of policing to combat crime over time because crime may decrease. If such a decrease occurs, the police could perform other tasks.

A key question pertains to whether legitimacy can link the police more directly to the goal of promoting community development. What is community development? Tyler and Jackson (2014) distinguish between psychological and behavioral indicators of development. Psychological indicators include identification with one's community and perceived social capital, while behavioral indicators include involvement in social activities (e.g., visit or talk to neighbors) and engaging in economic (shopping, seeking entertainment in the neighborhood) and political (attending neighborhood meetings, talking to local officials) activities.

Two arguments can be made here. The first is that a legitimate police force enables development by providing underlying reassurance. The second is that a legitimate police force promotes certain factors in the community, such as social capital, which subsequently promote community development.

5.1 Promoting Reassurance

In conjunction with the New York City Mayor's Office of Community Development, a survey of New York residents was conducted to test the reassurance argument. Our findings indicate that when the police are viewed as legitimate, community residents feel more reassured, less anxious, and safer. These feelings, in turn, lead people to be willing to cooperate with the police in fighting crime. On the other hand, these same feelings do not lead to heightened social capital or greater engagement with the community.

5.2 Strengthening Communities

The police can also encourage other factors that shape development. One of the most frequently mentioned community-focused factors is social capital, which is a feature of the community rather than the police. Social capital has been variously described as assisting the effective functioning of social groups by establishing better interpersonal relationships, a shared sense of identity, a shared understanding of community issues, shared norms, shared values, greater trust, more cooperation, and more openness via reciprocity. The central hypothesis in this context is that higher social capital predicts better community outcomes (safety, education, health, employment).

The elements of collective efficacy include trust in others and social bonds among neighbors (social cohesion). Shared expectations or norms are also important. If community members do not trust one another (i.e., if they exhibit low social cohesion) or do not have shared norms/values, then the community is not cohesive. Separately, people are less likely to participate in collective efforts to manage their communities (collective efficacy). It is suggested that it is important for a person to feel that others in the community are also willing to take action to maintain social order.

Sampson, Raudenbush, and Earls (1997) discuss collective efficacy, one element of social capital; this refers to the collective belief of neighbors that they are willing to intervene and control the behavior of others for the common good. Whether people believe that such a capacity exists in their neighborhood shapes community development.

It is important to distinguish between the belief that people in the community share norms and values and the legitimacy-based indicator of normative alignment, which suggests that people believe the police share their norms and values. Social capital is a feature of the people within the community.

Herbert (2006) highlights the importance of this perceived ability to rely on neighbors for assistance and he argues that living in a community with this type of social bond promotes a shared commitment to the neighborhood and is important to engagement. He claims that two aspects of the community are potentially valuable: perceptions of collective efficacy and the existence of a shared commitment to the community.

Seeking to summarize the social capital perspective based on a literature review, Scrivens and Smith (2013) outline four elements of social capital – i.e., personal relationships, social network support, civic engagement, and trust in others/having cooperative norms. Each of these elements plays a distinct role in community vitality, and each can be measured via surveys.

5.3 Social Capital in New York City

What is the connection between police legitimacy and community development? Tyler and Jackson (2014) focus on data drawn from a national survey in which 1,603 respondents completed an online questionnaire examining the role of the police in motivating engagement in communities. The results demonstrate that the legitimacy of the police/courts facilitates political, economic, and social engagement. Legitimacy has a direct influence on community identification and perceived social capital. It indirectly influences political and economic activity via its impact on community identification. In addition, if social capital is higher, residents are more willing to help the police fight crime.

The relationship is also examined in a survey of New Yorkers conducted by the Justice Collaboratory and sponsored by the Mayor's Office of Criminal Justice (MOCJ) in New York City (Tyler & Meares, 2021). This study is based on interviews with a random sample of the New York City residents. It considers the factors that shape people's engagement in activities that promote economic, political, and social development as well as their willingness to cooperate with the police. The New York study replicates the finding that legitimacy promotes people's willingness to help the police and that procedural justice shapes legitimacy. It further indicates that increased police legitimacy is associated with higher social capital. The key finding is that police legitimacy facilitates community development by promoting social capital because the latter is associated with economic, political, and social development.

On the other hand, the same study indicates that social capital does not significantly shape legitimacy. The strength of the relationships among neighbors does not affect views regarding the legitimacy of the police. So, trust in the police shapes the nature of the community, but that influence is not reciprocal. Police legitimacy flows from judgments about police procedural justice.

Yesberg and Bradford (2021) also evaluate the social capital and policing literature. They note that the mechanisms by which policing shapes collective efficacy are not well understood. However, one antecedent that they identify as supported by the research is legitimacy. Their review highlights studies that link trust in the police to collective efficacy and community engagement (Kochel, 2012). A separation of legitimacy into its constitutive elements in the MOCJ sample shows that trust and normative alignment have the strongest impacts on collective efficacy, while obligation influences cooperation with the police.

These findings suggest a role for the police that continues to be relevant even as crime rates decline. To enable this valuable role, policing must change. The style of policing must shift from a warrior model to a service model. The procedural justice that people experience when dealing with the police should be enhanced. To the degree that the police embrace these changes, they play an important role in facilitating community development and thus in the task of encouraging more vital communities.

The argument that the police can play a vital role in community development, and that this role is important irrespective of the crime rate, is an argument that supports maintaining current police departments while simultaneously rethinking their mission and culture. If the police become more service-oriented and emphasize procedural justice–based policing, they can maintain and develop their legitimacy while controlling crime. And while they are controlling crime, they can also reassure community residents and simultaneously promote the economic, social, and political development of neighborhoods.

In other words, the police can adopt a legitimacy-based approach to policing because it facilitates controlling crime *and* simultaneously promotes community development. The goals of reducing harm and promoting community vitality can be approached at the same time.

5.4 How Should Resources Be Allocated?

The fact that the police can help facilitate community development does not demonstrate that maintaining current police levels, but retraining police officers in accordance with a service framework, is the best use of available resources. It should be considered whether it would be better to reallocate resources away from the police. Funding the police vs. funding other services is a trade-off.

One way of thinking about trade-offs is in terms of balancing different skill sets within police departments to achieve the goal of creating and sustaining legitimacy while managing issues related to crime control and community development. A different way of considering trade-offs is highlighted by research conducted by Chalfin and McCrary (2017, 2018). This work is frequently cited because it provides data suggesting that hiring more police lowers crime rates. This effect differs across crimes but is consistently significant (Chalfin & McCrary, 2018). The authors' analysis focuses on murder, which, they argue, is associated with much higher costs than property crime. They suggest that this supports the importance of maintaining or even enlarging traditional police forces.

We discuss Chalfin and McCrary (2017), because they advocate a different (and, we think, helpful) approach to addressing crime. Even if hiring additional police officers lowers crime, could it be reasonable not to increase police numbers, And if so, why? The underlying question pertains to the ways in which a municipality can best spend its money. It could be true that hiring more police officers is efficacious in reducing crime, but it may not be the best use of a city's money. An analysis by Chalfin and McCrary (2017) compares investments in more police to other uses of a similar amount of money. If you have $1,000,000, how might you best invest it? The argument proposed by these authors suggests that changing labor conditions also influences crime, so that money might alternatively be invested in job creation.

What is the best approach to managing crime? It is first important to explicate the question. Discussions of policing typically merely argue for hiring police officers to address crime, but financial trade-offs are actually involved in this process. Chalfin and McCrary highlight the distinction between violent crime and property crime. Murder, for example, costs society a great deal, so it makes sense to spend a considerable amount of money in order to lower the murder rate. Property crime, however, is less costly. The review by Chalfin and McCrary (2017, p. 35) suggests that aggregate unemployment has an important impact on property crime, thus suggesting that alternative approaches may be effective in lowering the rate of property crime. Several studies suggest that higher average wages lower rates of both property crime and crime (one study reports an elasticity ranging between -0.3 to -0.9; see Chalfin and McCrary [2017]). In contrast, the elasticity for hiring police officers is -0.4.

The key point is that we should not make the assumption that hiring more police is the best use of municipal resources. The best use of money might be creating jobs. Chalfin and McCrary highlight many caveats and assumptions that are made with respect to these types of analyses. However, the point is that it can be claimed that the best way of controlling crime is not inevitably related to more policing, even if policing does lower the rate of crime. Another way to spend money is by focusing on the pursuit of a new goal – building community vitality. This goal involves spending money on economic and social growth. Of course, spending money on both goals is the best solution, but one that often conflicts with limited municipal budgets.

A concrete example of a cost–benefit approach is retraining, as can be seen in the case of those in the community who are mentally ill. Police departments widely regard this issue as important and provide specialized training for officers. Does this approach address the problem? To some degree, better trained officers, alongside policies focused on diversion to social services, provide a better solution to the issue of managing mental illness in communities than the current approach of sending traditionally trained officers. Simultaneously, recent discussions have emphasized that a more desirable solution to the issue may be to develop and utilize community-based assertive outreach (Watson, Compton, & Pope, 2019). Like proactive policing, this approach tries to preempt problems, but it minimizes the role played by law enforcement. It does so by focusing on community-based social services agencies rather than the police. In this case, the argument is that retraining the police is not clearly the most desirable way of providing mental health services. The best approach may be to shift funding to nonpolice responses. This approach can be contrasted with a joint response model that, whatever its benefits, raises costs by requiring a police officer and a social service worker to be present at every response (see Lavoie, Alvarez, & Kandil, 2022).

Trade-offs can also be conceptualized in another way, namely, as a trade-off between police presence and legitimacy costs. As Owens and Ba (2021) suggest, police intrusions in people's lives have legitimacy costs, especially if they experience such intrusions as illegitimate. Rather than evaluating proactive policing solely in terms of crime control, it is important to balance that factor against the crime creation that results from decreased trust in the police. This point is highlighted by the finding that one of the consequences of the costs associated with maintaining high numbers of police officers is that many police departments generate their funding through widespread fines connected with police stops. Thus, the need to create funding motivates illegitimate stops and fines (McIntire & Keller, 2021). This situation is a cost associated with maintaining the police in their present numbers. If the number of police officers were reduced, the pressure to generate these revenues would diminish. In other words, having the police requires funding the police, and the way in which such funding is ensured can undermine other goals.

6 Expanding Participation When Identifying Community Problems and Solutions

In the previous section, we outlined the advantages of using legitimacy-based policing as a model for expanding the goals of policing. In this section, we focus on the possibility of reorganizing the ways in which communities think about managing community problems by broadening our understanding of procedural justice. In the policing literature, procedural justice has been almost entirely conceptualized as focusing on reactions to the implementation of police actions in the community; however, the same principles of procedural justice can be (and, in other arenas, have been) applied to the creation of institutions and their policies and practices.

The arena of American policing would seem to be an ideal context for greater citizen involvement because the structure of American legal authority locates policing authority at the local community level. This characteristic is distinctly American, since many societies have strong national police forces. In addition, this highlights the irony that, in contrast to the view that local authority facilitates governance, American police are less trusted by their communities than are police in many societies with national forces. Nonetheless, at least in theory, localism facilitates responsiveness to the community.

One reason to think that citizen participation might work well at the community level is that Americans have more trust in local authorities than in state or national authorities. A 2021 Gallup poll indicates that 39 percent of Americans trust the federal government to handle domestic problems, 57 percent trust state governments, and 66 percent trust their local governments (Brenan, 2021b). The local community level is also where the public has the most extensive personal experience, as well as offering the most significant possibilities for participation and involvement.

Finally, this argument fits with a new emphasis on localism, i.e., change at the local community level. An example of this emphasis is the argument by Katz and Nowak (2018) in *The new localism* suggesting that change in our current era of mistrust in institutions can best occur via local communities. An example of the application of this approach is outlined by Spade (2020), who advocates mutual aid among different people in local communities to make joint efforts to solve local problems.

Involving communities more fully in decisions regarding ways of creating the conditions necessary for safety involves three issues. The first is identifying what people in the community view as their needs and goals. Most discussions of policing begin with existing departments and ask what the community wants these departments to do. Our focus is on the possibility of taking a step back from that question to ask what people in the communities believe they need and to inquire into the ways in which those needs can best be addressed. This approach allows the design of policing to flow from community needs rather than police concerns serving as the beginning point of the discussion.

The second issue pertains to the development of procedures for aggregating individual views into a community consensus regarding desirable policies and practices. This approach represents the most direct extension of the ideas of procedural justice, but in this case procedures are aimed at determining what policies should be created rather than examining whether predetermined policies are being implemented fairly. This task involves some form of deliberation or consensus building.

The third issue focuses on ways of combining input from community views with the expertise and experience of the police to create a framework that can address the needs of the community most effectively. As noted, procedural justice–based models for establishing institutions and defining policies and practices serve as one model that can guide this effort.

6.1 A Community-Based Effort toward Institutional Design

Rather than accepting the existing model of policing, an alternative theoretical model can be articulated and supported. This model does not focus on reforming existing institutions – rather, it argues that the system should be reimagined to allow us to rethink our goals and thereby promote institutional redesign. To address this question, we must begin by taking a step back from policing and crime to ask a more fundamental question: What are the problems in the community, and how can these problems best be addressed? We can take this approach as an alternative to merely accepting existing criminal legal institutions and asking how they can be reformed. As Bell (2021, p. 1) argues, it is important to "disentangle policing from public safety" and to avoiding falling into a pattern of "responding to concerns about public safety with status quo policing, perhaps with a few tweaks to existing training and practices."

Many contemporary reform efforts are inevitably limited because they begin by accepting the premises of the existing criminal legal system, when it is those very premises that cause the problems that reformers are trying to solve. A fundamental reimagining is necessary to address these issues.

As an example, consider the action of a group of fathers in response to the presence of fighting in schools in their community (Karimi & Lemos, 2021). This phenomenon is a social order problem that is normally handled in a reflexive manner by increasing the intervention of either school authorities or the police and defined as a problem of rule enforcement associated with the sanctioning and exclusion of troublemakers (Tyler & Trinkner, 2018). In this community, a group of fathers decided to step in and serve as informal counselors and managers of conflict at their children's school. Setting aside the many issues with this process in terms of scalability and sustainability, the point is that it is possible to develop and implement community-created and organized solutions to problems that would typically be addressed by the criminal legal system.

Another example of the ways in which community involvement can change the conceptualization of problems is highlighted by Gohara's (2022) study of the desires of Black crime victims. She notes that rather than focusing on the individualist-retributive model of the criminal legal system, Black-led victim organizations take a more restorative approach and emphasize the need for services to address poverty. Her analysis contrasts this minority-led effort with the development of victim groups in White communities, which focus on the punishment of individual criminals.

The first example cited above illustrates an effort by people within a community to collaborate to address a problem, i.e., it reflects the essence of collective efficacy. The second example illustrates the role that community groups play in addressing legal issues via a community framework that may or may not direct problems to the legal system for resolution. Neither of these approaches is a new phenomenon in the United States. Early in the country's history, de Tocqueville (2000) highlighted the tendency of people in American communities to collaborate to solve their problems rather than turning to the government. That propensity is enshrined in the US Constitution, which is based on the idea of local democratic experimentalism (Dorf & Sabel, 1998), whose capacity is blunted when local elites take control of decision-making and broad participation is not encouraged.

In recent years, the problem of such a reimagining has been confounded with the challenges associated with the inclusion of community voices in discussions pertaining to ways of managing community problems. As noted, the police tend to assume authority and create a police-centered framework for discussing change. The command-and-control approach projects policies and practices onto communities. And policies and practices are defined by the police based on their expertise. The police may seek to hold meetings with the community, but a common complaint is that these community meetings represent an attempt by the police to direct the actions of the community and define local agendas (Cheng, 2020).

How should we assess community needs? One place to seek guidance is the literature pertaining to the legal needs of the public. There is a great deal of literature concerning the problems that people experience in their lives that might be relevant to law. Obviously, not all needs are connected to law or the police, but the methodology used in this context is illustrative of the ways in which the problem of assessing needs might advance.

The classic study of legal needs is Curran (1977). This study of a sample of Americans begins by identifying the types of problems that people encounter in their lives: real estate, employment, consumer issues, deaths, marital problems, issues with government agencies, torts, criminal conduct, and rights infringements

(Currie, 2009). A key finding is that people typically do not view many of the problems they experience in everyday life as legal problems, and they often seek informal ways of resolving them. This tendency illustrates the point that an analysis that begins by identifying problems often does not lead individuals to seek help from a government entity, i.e., in this case, usually going to a civil court.

A recent article by Sandefur (2015) discusses the question of what people want when they experience problems in their lives. An enormous number of problems are traditionally defined as "legal" in the sense that lawyers believe that they are actionable within the framework of the courts. These problems involve issues such as health, housing, and employment, which are central to making communities vital, and their effective resolution shapes the quality of people's lives. An interesting finding of research concerning legal needs high-lights the low degree of relevance that law has to people's understanding of most of their everyday problems. The research suggests that when Americans are asked about their experiences with such problems or situations, they often do not think of their justice-related problems in legal terms (Sandefur, 2012). To address most of those problems, people tend to do little or nothing either in legal terms or in other ways, an approach that is often known as "lumping it"; the salient question is why this tendency exists. Sandefur (2015) suggests that the problem that people experience is not the issue of limited access to law and legal services. She notes that cost issues are not the primary reason why people refrain from contacting lawyers. Rather, they do not view the legal system as a path to justice.

The analogy to policing is direct. A key change that is necessary in the context of policing requires us to consider how policing would change if we were to define systems in terms of the concerns of users rather than those of the legal authorities. The key is to begin with the problems that people face and build on that foundation to define possible solutions, which might involve neighbors or community groups.

Typically, people look to others in their communities, either by talking directly to those involved or by going to a neighbor, friend, minister, or local community group leader to help them solve their problems. Similarly, many everyday problems can be, and are, solved informally. The social capital scale, as one example, focuses on collaboration among neighbors. This scale asks questions such as "If children on the street are making trouble, would you intervene?" or "Would your neighbors intervene?" rather than "Would you call the police?"

In parallel with the legal system, police authorities argue that traditional police services represent the solution to many everyday problems. As in the case of the courts, it is possible that people do not share this view in many cases. The key is to ask what types of procedures for meeting needs, managing problems, resolving conflicts, and regulating conduct lead people – disputants, offenders, victims, and the general population of a community – to feel that appropriate mechanisms are available for maintaining social order and promoting community vitality. This process can involve legal authorities, the police, and the courts, but it can also involve many other individuals, institutions, and organizations.[7]

These approaches argue that the key issue is to address the needs of people and the communities in which they live. It is important to build on the foundation of those needs to reach solutions rather than assuming that existing institutions represent the best way of meeting people's needs. It is also important to recognize that those needs may be different than often imagined. On the other hand, people may want and value many traditional services, including those provided by the police. Thus, it is possible that an analysis that begins with the identification of community needs would replicate many of the types of governmental services that already exist.

6.2 What Do People Want?

One way of thinking about community input is that it is already present because policing is local in nature and people can, and do, elect their local leaders. Those leaders then represent their communities. An issue that has arisen in the context of policing is the suggestion that some elements of the community have been excluded from discussions and have had their concerns undervalued. This view is best represented in the literature concerning the policing of Black communities, which are suggested to be overpoliced and underserved by the police.

How can community views be collected? There are two distinct ways of incorporating community input into policy design. One way is via interviews with a diverse and representative sample of community members. The second way is to use some kind of forum to gather views from the community. An example of this process is a portal; another example is Community Based Participation Action Research (CBPAR).

Assessing public views via interviews brings the strengths and weaknesses of a key methodology in the social sciences to bear on the task of defining

---

[7] This approach leads to the idea of institutional design. Bingham (2008, p. 9) suggests that organizations, institutions, and forums should be designed by reference to their capacity to meet individual and group needs. The capacities of different approaches to advance personal and communal goals must be systematically compared. As Bingham (2008) argues, "Without the capacity to undertake systematic, comparative institutional assessments, recommendations of reform may be based on naïve ideas about what kinds of institutions are good or bad and not on an analysis of performance."

a community consensus with respect to issues pertaining to social order. One conceptual issue revolves around ways of identifying the people from whom the data are to be collected. Some form of random choice is often utilized in this context, but there are many ways of attempting to obtain a diverse sample. A second issue pertains to whether the data collection is to involve in-person interviews or some form of questionnaire. Either form of data collection can be open-ended or use a closed response format.

It is also possible to identify stakeholders who care more about a particular issue. This approach is often enacted by default when there are community meetings and they address the concerns of the people who show up. If people in communities feel alienated from government or from their own community they are less inclined to proactively involve themselves in efforts to govern. This, in turn, ensures that their concerns are underrepresented in discussions about community issues.

6.3 Portals

Portals are a new approach to capturing first-hand accounts of policing in American cities. They are immersive audiovisual environments that allow distant people to talk as if they were in the same room. By introducing people from different communities and prompting dialogues about the police, researchers can "remove themselves from the conversation," thus creating a space in which citizens can express their opinions freely. Instead, local community members called curators facilitate the dialogues — sometimes by guiding the conversation, other times by taking part.

Portal dialogues suggest several conclusions (Prowse, Weaver, & Meares, 2019). One is that an arrangement of "distorted responsiveness" characterizes the relationship between policed communities and the state. The police are viewed as overregulating and underserving the community. A second argument is that the political desire of policed communities is not simply for greater engagement along traditional lines but rather for political recognition – to have concerns acknowledged and acted upon by the state. The results of these studies suggest that people feel that the state has too much presence in their communities while, at the same time, they have too little power vis-à-vis state representatives. Finally, the authors argue that people follow an "ethics of aversion" in their political responses, i.e., they hold the belief that power is best achieved by withdrawing from state institutions in the short term and forging their own collective, autonomous community in the long term.

Other recent reforms have focused on the concept of CBPAR. This is a collaborative approach to research that involves all stakeholders throughout the entire research process, from establishing the research question, to developing data collection tools, and to the analysis and dissemination of findings. The idea is that this process transforms all members of the community into genuine partners. The approach gives people a voice in identifying and solving the social problems that affect their communities. It explicitly focuses on community-based organizations that bring together community members to visualize and actualize research and its outcomes. This includes nonprofit organizations that operate in specific local communities and are staffed by, work with, represent, assist, and/or advocate on behalf of the residents of those communities with respect to issues that affect their quality of life. These organizations work to gain trust among community members and bring together a spectrum of people with varying ideas and perspectives that focus on a particular set of concerns that are relevant to a large portion of the community. The idea is to support these organizations, whose work directly engages community members in creating change.

The factor that unites these approaches is the goal of improving the engagement of communities in discussions regarding their future. The underlying premise is that the carceral experience of being policed and, in particular, sanctioned with incarceration, leads to widespread alienation and withdrawal from community activity (Ang & Tebes, 2021; Brayne, 2014; Lerman & Weaver, 2014; Soss & Weaver, 2017). Proactive efforts are needed to overcome this withdrawal and those efforts need to involve the development of mechanisms for authentic participation.

In a democracy, arguing that the community should be involved in deciding how social order should be maintained is not unreasonable. In fact, given the amount of contemporary discussion in the political arena concerning government policies and how governments should function, it is striking how little discussion takes place concerning the appropriate form of criminal law. Such discussion could both enhance the likelihood that policies will reflect community views and promote feelings of ownership with respect to whatever policies and practices emerge as consensus choices. In addition, giving a voice to a broader section of the community might bring forward new ideas and perspectives and result in policies that better address collective needs.

One important precursor underlying this argument is the need to stop thinking of poor or minority communities as fundamentally damaged or pathological. Scholarship pertaining to such communities emphasizes the fact that despite the economic disadvantages or social exclusion imposed by larger society, such communities have been and continue to be dynamic and vital both in terms of economic activity (Parker, 2015) and social activity and culture (Alexander, 2012; Hunter, 2010; Hunter et al., 2016).

6.4 Building Consensus

Irrespective of the manner in which information is collected, it is necessary to develop some method of distilling diverse views into a consensus. The most frequently recognized issue in this context is the difference between majority and minority community views. Trust in the police is much lower among Black residents and in Black communities, which reflect a minority of the general population (approximately 13 percent of the American population is Black according to the 2020 Census).

In addition, disagreement within communities is a frequent phenomenon. A particularly important finding reported by studies concerning minority communities is that those communities do not necessarily oppose the idea of the police playing a substantial role. Forman (2017), for example, documents support for prison sentences among members of the minority community in Washington, DC. And Bell (2016) outlines the conflicts that minority group members living in poor communities face when balancing their desire for police services against their distrust of the police. Public opinion is complex in all communities.

A second issue is the task of defining procedures for public deliberation. These procedures must be legitimate both according to those involved and the broader community. Key to that legitimacy is procedural justice. Procedural justice is often associated with authority relations, but it also applies to bilateral procedures such as negotiation and group processes like deliberation. Given the realities of community size, deliberation typically involves representatives from different groups. These representatives may or may not include forums for input from others in the community as part of their procedures. The realities of deliberation mirror the realities of representative democracy, a system of decision-making that recognizes that it is unrealistic for everyone in a community to participate in governance and thus assigns that task to representatives.

A variety of procedural issues is raised by deliberation. The first pertains to the way in which the people involved are chosen and whether they reflect the entire community (Levine, 2016). In the past, in the case of policing, there have been persistent cases in which unheard voices are excluded from participation. It is often the case that community leaders – for example, church leaders – step forward to represent a community, which may or may not lead to the inclusion of everyone.

The second issue pertains to the procedure by which deliberation occurs. The process of evaluating procedures raises issues concerning whether everyone has voice, whether all sides are represented, and whether decisions are made in an open, unbiased, and fact-based manner. As in the case of most community-based procedures, the parties may not enter the deliberation with equal resources and power, and they may differ in terms of their levels of expertise and experience. All these issues influence whether a consensus is reached and, if it is, whether the various parties involved in the deliberation and in the community they represent view this consensus as legitimate.

Discussions of democratic deliberation can be considered by reference to the framework developed by Habermas (1989; see Held, 2006). That framework emphasizes (1) the inclusion of all people; (2) civil and well-informed constructive dialogue; and (3) ideal role-taking, according to which people are encouraged to consider problems from the perspectives of others. As such, this approach has many similarities with a procedural justice approach.

One area in which attention has been given to procedural justice in deliberation is environmental regulation. A particular concern of procedural justice has been the participation of community residents in decisions regarding conservation and other environmental issues. It has been noted that the public increasingly do not trust elites, including both governmental and scientific authorities (Kellstedt, Zahran, & Vedlitz, 2008; Poortinga & Pidgeon, 2003), to make such decisions and seek to play a meaningful role in decision-making procedures (Kaase, 1999; Lorenzoni & Pidgeon, 2006; Lubell et al., 2006). These procedures include those related to wildlife management (Lacey, Edwards, & Lamont, 2016), forest management (Lacey, Edwards, & Lamont, 2016), and many other issues. The key unifying theme in this context is that "The effectiveness of collaborative environmental decision-making processes hinges on the degree to which participating stakeholder groups (i.e., policy actors) perceive their processes to be fair" (Hamilton, 2018, p. xx). This theme includes the willingness to reach agreements and accept them (Winter & May, 2001).

The ideas of procedural justice provide a framework for deliberation within communities focused on identifying a set of widely endorsed "consensus" policies regarding a shared set of mechanisms to promote social order. Such discussion does not necessarily lead to an argument in support of defunding the police. Clearly, some segments of the community want more of the same type of policing that we now have. And this group includes certain segments of poor and minority communities. There are arguments for overpolicing and underpolicing in most communities. As we have already noted, these discussions about how much policing is desirable are intertwined with issues about how existing police exercise their authority.

O'Brien, Tyler, and Meares (2019) suggest actions in which the police can engage to facilitate deliberation. One such action is the creation of additional participatory opportunities at the community level. Another is the employment of reconciliatory gestures that bring various parties together. Jonathan-

Zamir, Perry, and Weisburd (2020) highlight ways in which the police can create community-level opportunities for deliberation. As noted, the police can facilitate deliberation, but they need not necessarily be central to this process. Local groups can also work on their own and/or with a variety of government agencies. The key point in this context is that community-based deliberation facilitated by community-level procedures are experienced as fair. A variety of types of forums for deliberation have been identified and tested, ranging from community meetings (Fishkin, 1991) to referendums. These forums focus particularly on the goal of providing a voice to the community.

In addition to encouraging people to feel that policies are created in just ways, community involvement enables people in those communities to participate, improves their civic competence, increases their participatory knowledge and skills, and facilitates rational decision-making (Curato et al., 2017; Farrell, O'Malley, & Suiter, 2013; Grönlund, Setälä, & Herne, 2010). The CBPAR appraoch has already been noted. A goal in involving the community at all stages is to develop its capacity to make decisions about its own future. As it stands today, many communities have trouble sustaining efforts to chart their future and the police often step in and direct those efforts. But, when the police direct such discussions, community capacity to work collectively is not developed and, if people feel excluded, the community becomes more alienated and less able to work toward a consensus.

A common feature of these approaches is the recognition that they need to occur over time and can involve multiple stages. As an example, an opinion poll using a random sample can be followed by in- person deliberation. It is beyond the scope of this Element to review the literature on possible forms of deliberation and consensus-building within communities. While different in many ways, they all share the goal of taking the many voices within a community and arriving at a consensus that will be broadly accepted. This literature suggests that acceptance is influenced by views about the justice of the deliberation procedure, as distinct from its outcomes.

6.5 Expertise vs. Experience

Even if it were possible to distill community views, the issue of managing expertise vs. community views must also be considered. The police are experts and are often deferred to in the context of making decisions regarding public policy. If the police are responsive to the public in terms of the way in which they implement those policies, they are both managing crime and contributing to community development. It is reasonable to ask why communities would benefit if police views were supplanted by community views regarding the way in which municipal resources should be allocated. This question is particularly salient because public views are frequently recognized as uninformed and based on a misunderstanding of the facts surrounding community problems.

Public views are driven by the crisis of the moment. Poor public policies that have been inspired by moral panics range from three-strikes laws to sexual registry regulations. In the field of policing, the gap between actual and perceived crime rates is widely documented, allowing political leaders to exploit unjustified fears. A mechanism must be developed to ensure that when the views of the public are taken into consideration, ways of evaluating the probative value (i.e., accuracy) of those views are also available. Recognition of the potential value of indicators of development and vitality, in addition to public opinion, returns the discussion to the need for reform efforts to combine the experience and expertise of community and police leaders with the views of the public.

Krauss et al. (2021, 2022) refer to public reactions to immediate events as crime control theater. These authors suggest that the public holds many views regarding what works. and these may differ from empirical findings though they are nevertheless important politically. Recently, Goff, Swencionis, and Tyler (2022) demonstrated that public support for sanctions, versus support for alternatives such as treatment, are based on public views concerning the relative efficacy of these alternative approaches with respect to addressing the problem of crime. Part of what is important is a change in public awareness of effective alternatives to force-based models of crime control.

Goff, Swencionis, and Tyler (2022) demonstrate that people are actually less supportive of force-based responses to crime than they are of approaches such as restorative justice and community development. They regard such nonforce-based solutions as more likely to be effective. It is therefore troubling that perceptions of a crime wave seem to be most commonly associated with calls for more traditional force-based policing. This reflexive connection of violent crime threats to the need for more traditional policing is an aspect of crime control theater. As noted, traditional force-based policing can influence crime. However, research suggests that this approach is not superior to other approaches and has clear negative aspects. Perhaps most prominent in this context is the fact that it is a strategy of crime suppression. It is particularly successful at immediate, short-term suppression. However, its lack of long-term impact means that it perpetuates the cycle of responding to dramatic criminal acts by calls to increase the presence of existing police forces.

An important aspect of the findings of Goff, Swencionis, and Tyler (2022) is that when respondents view the police as legitimate, they are more likely to believe that both sanction-based and treatment-based policies are effective in both preventing crime and dealing with crime after it occurs. This finding suggests that a public that trusts the police believe that the police are able to make noncoercive approaches effective in managing crime. Simultaneously, legitimacy also causes the public to be more supportive of the proposition to give the police authority to use force. Essentially, legitimacy supports discretion, with the public endorsing both sanction-based and treatment-based approaches to crime. The treatment approaches to crime include those that are immediate, such as mediation, and longer-term approaches, including community service, job placement programs, job training, and drug treatment.

Furthermore, it is possible to directly compare public views of the two models of policing that we are considering. One approach that can be considered is the development of trust in the police. In a national sample (Goff, Swencionis, & Tyler, 2022), 64 percent of respondents indicated that they believe that the legitimacy-based model is effective in lowering crime. In contrast, 27 percent claimed that widespread police stops are effective, 22 percent believed that sanctioning by the police is effective, and 41 percent maintained that postcrime punishment via imprisonment deters crime. Overall, the public are more supportive of legitimacy-based policing than sanctioning, believing it to be a more effective way of managing crime. Both overall, and in specific terms, the public are in favor of approaches to crime that are community- and treatment-oriented and aim at improving police legitimacy.

A core problem with public views is that fear of crime and perceptions of the crime rate are not obviously correlated with actual rates of crime (Owens & Ba, 2021). Hence, perceptions constitute a distinct reality, and whether or not the police do lower the actual rate of crime, this effect may or may not change evaluations of the problem of crime. This claim is particularly true with respect to violent crimes, which are highly visible. A single violent crime may gain widespread attention from the media but does little or nothing to alter the probability of the everyday resident becoming a victim.

Irrespective of the quality of public opinion, efforts to develop a cooperative relationship with communities, based on an attempt to respond to community views, require engaging with public perceptions. This task may involve developing ways of bringing those perceptions more in line with reality. It is difficult to determine whether the public exhibits a poor understanding of crime because they have not been involved in efforts to manage it, and/or whether the lack of community capacity to develop a consensus reflects previous exclusion from the policy creation process.

One way of improving community involvement is to encourage greater participation by the public in decision-making, which improves their capacity to make rational decisions regarding public policy issues. Discussions of community deliberation emphasize that is not a quick process. People need time to become educated about the issues and to become familiar with different points of view. This task is not necessarily something in which everyone in the community can be involved. However, it is something that group representatives can do and subsequently communicate to their constituents.

As noted, the public and the police do not always agree about which policing problems are important (Higgins, 2019). Similarly, studies suggest that the public, public officials, and experts often disagree about how community well-being should be measured (Kim, Kee, & Lee, 2015). This finding indicates that some deliberative process to reconcile differences must be implemented. As mentioned, the topic of how communities can deliberate to address problems collectively is not new to social science (see Bohman & Rehg, 1997; Fung, 2004; Parkinson & Mansbridge, 2012).

As we have noted, there is a robust literature on deliberation. A recent review of that literature suggested several optimistic conclusions (Dryzek et al., 2019). First, research "offers reasons for optimism about citizens' capacity to avoid polarization and manipulation and make sound decisions" (Dryzek et al., 2019, p. 1144) in community deliberations. Second, "Deliberative experimentation has generated empirical research that refutes many of the more pessimistic claims about the citizenry's ability to make sound judgments" (Dryzek et al., 2019, p. 1145) during deliberations. This supports the suggestion that more inclusive community decision-making is both feasible and desirable in many settings.

6.6 Community Pressure for Change

The counterpoint to a critique of the public is the recognition that the police have been slow to change in response to changing circumstances. There is no greater indication of this fact than the finding that while crime has been declining steadily for decades, police funding has remained more or less stable since the 1980s. Similarly, although the problems that the police encounter have become more oriented toward social work, police forces have resisted retraining.

Notwithstanding the problems with public opinion, successful changes in policing typically only occur when there is sustained public pressure for change. As Canales (2022a, 2022b) suggests, the community must "own" the reform movement. His work suggests that in the absence of sustained community pressure, policing defaults to a coercive model. Hence, whatever the problems with the public's views, public pressure is essential to change. This finding suggests that an important topic for the future is the task of determining how to increase the capacity of the community to collectively support ideas that are fact-based and sustainable. This must involve giving the community actual ownership of key aspects of decision-making; in other words, there needs to be active community engagement and a true allocation of responsibility for some issues to people in the community.

At the same time, Canales highlights that successful reform requires both sustained community pressure and the willingness to make changes in police departments. As he notes in the context of reform in Stockton, California connected to Operation Ceasefire (a program focused on reducing gun violence),

> dedicated efforts to empower clients emerged in parallel to a city-wide emphasis on procedural justice training, where the lesson that human beings must be treated as ends, and not merely objects to be acted on, was deeply instilled. In that sense, in parallel to testing new mechanisms to deliver the Ceasefire message, the partners have attempted to increasingly draw clients into the conversations and carve out new spaces for their voices. (Canales, 2022c, p. 44).

He further comments that part of this transformation required changes to make the police more open to the community: "For a city that had long relied on place-based and zero-tolerance enforcement, transitioning towards ... direct communication with, and ultimately, the empowerment of ... individuals proved counterintuitive. Procedural justice, on the other hand, offered a simple and intuitive mechanism to gradually instill these practices within the department" (Canales, 2022c, p. 50). As these comments suggest, an emphasis on procedural justice gradually transforms the process of community management into a more inclusive and deliberative process, but that transition requires changes within both the community and the police department.

Canales makes a similar observation with respect to the implementation of violence reduction in Oakland, California as part of Operation Ceasefire (Canales, 2022b). He notes that "Oakland Ceasefire had several complementarities with other organizational processes such as recruiting training, analysis, and intelligence-gathering. It is worth unpacking its exceptional complementarity with procedural justice. Attempting a successful intervention of Ceasefire may require the parallel or prior implementation of procedural justice principles" (Canales, 2022b, p. 17) Again, part of the process of change in this case involved a transformation in the police department, while another part involved a transformation in the community; these two processes occurred in tandem. At both levels, transformation was facilitated by adopting a community-level approach to procedural justice.

These case studies illustrate the parallel issues in communities and police departments. The first is that sustained efforts to make changes develop out of communities that can engage in collective deliberation and support sustained change efforts. Those communities are more likely to be successful when their police departments have themselves adopted a procedural model. A police department that is based upon procedural justice is more likely to connect and work well with a community that is developing its own mechanisms for identifying priorities and organizing to promote social change. It is also important to accept that change inevitably unfolds over time.

These examples also illustrate the reality that efforts at social change inevitably require communities to both define their own goals and needs and work in cooperation with existing institutions such as the police. It is challenging to try to step back from existing institutions and reimagine social order, and it is a political problem to try to introduce new ideas into the community if the agencies have not themselves transformed to be more open and responsive to community voices.

6.7 External Metrics of Development

The goal of development at the community level is community vitality, while at the individual level, it is the flourishing of the people within the community. The absence of harm is not identical with the presence of vitality or flourishing. This issue ranges beyond the context of policing. Studies of communities often fail to distinguish between reducing harms such as mental illness or gun violence and enhancing the presence of well-being, compassion, and trust (Krekel et al., 2021).

Given the problems with relying on public opinion as a counterpoint to police expertise and police willingness to lead change, it is important to try to discover objective metrics of community vitality and individual well-being that we can use as a benchmark for development. These metrics can be objective in nature – for example, employment rates or wage levels – or they can be distinct psychological attributes identified by experts as desirable, for example, self-reported happiness.

An example of an effort to expand such evaluation criteria is the NeighborhoodStat effort of New York City's MOCJ (Bailey et al., 2016). This effort involves residents in a joint problem-solving process to define a set of criteria for community policies. Its scope is broad and includes attempts to define both objective and subjective indicators as metrics of community development. A large body of literature investigates ways of measuring desirable community policies, and a detailed discussion of this topic is beyond the scope of this Element. Our main point is that there are frameworks whose goal is to identify measurable indicators of community development (see Frijters & Krekel, 2021; Phillips & Wong, 2017).

6.8 Community Vitality as Economic Strength

A starting point for many discussions pertaining to vital communities is the task of developing a large stock of economic resources. In World Bank discussions, gross national product (GNP) is often the starting point in the task of analyzing a society's vitality. The community's standard of living is a metric of its vitality. Beyond the simple level of income or wealth lie the inequity-related questions of poverty and inequality. Poverty refers to the existence of substantial economic deprivation in at least some parts of a community. Inequality refers to an unequal distribution of wealth within a community or society. These discussions direct attention to indicators of general or concentrated poverty and resulting harms. These indicators include lower life expectancy, higher rates of child mortality, or even less access to water, sanitation, and electricity. Such metrics directly align development and greater vitality with material gains.

It is recognized that economic strength and well-being are not identical (Canadian Index of Wellbeing, 2016). Community vitality and individual well-being involves social relationships and support, social engagement, social norms and values, feelings regarding others, and feelings of belonging to one's community. Measuring vitality should include both objective and psychological indicators. Subjective indicators include a sense of belonging to the community, having friends, feeling that other people can be trusted, and not feeling that one is a victim of discrimination. Objective indicators include participating in unpaid volunteering and individual acts of helping others.

6.9 Vitality as Psychological Well-Being

Studies of vitality are often based on objective indicators. Like crime rates, these indicators are frequently readily available. However, another approach to understanding vitality is to conceptualize it in terms of subjective feelings. A core distinction is between those feelings that impact resilience/coping and those that affect flourishing (Krekel et al., 2021). Resilience refers to an individual's capacity to deal with stress, to adapt, and to engage in coping behavior. Flourishing is a positive statement regarding a person's mental health and engagement in his or her community. Similar to the community-level distinction between harm reduction and vitality, the ability to cope with trauma or disadvantage is not identical to the capacity to be satisfied and fulfilled, i.e., the promotion of human flourishing.

6.10 Why Support Community Engagement?

In Section 5 we noted that legitimacy-based policing allows the police to manage crime and promote community development at the same time. From this perspective, the police might ask why they should also promote greater empowerment of people in the community. As noted, such empowerment is central to sustained social change, but is there an argument that such change is needed or desirable if existing institutions are functioning in appropriate ways?

An important reason for supporting community empowerment is that it is another path toward stronger communities that is distinct from the impact of police legitimacy on social capital. Police legitimacy makes communities stronger in a variety of ways, but it does not necessarily create the ability to think about community goals and/or to learn how to listen to others, compromise, and accept shared decisions.

Studies of deliberation make clear that community empowerment is a way to improve the quality of decision-making, resolve divisive issues, and engage broad segments of the community. In an era of divisiveness, efforts to bring communities together are particularly important and the management of social order has long been one of the more potentially divisive issues.

While it matters in many arenas, the capacity to deliberate is especially important in respect of crime because it helps to make communities more sophisticated and less open to moral panics and political theater. Authentic opportunities for involvement create a public that can better deal with evidence-informed policing and governance. Examples of how ill-formed public views have led to suboptimal policies are plentiful in criminal law, so a more capable public is desirable.

A second reason to improve public capacity is that the police are not always right. Having acknowledged the expertise of the police, it is also important to recognize that policing is a profession and police departments are institutions. Like all professions and institutions they have blind spots and are subject to the type of "groupthink" social forces that can suppress dissent and stifle change – forces that are recognized to be very strong in police departments. If the community is involved in deliberation there are external voices. This is not to say that communities do not have their own blind spots, but balancing forces provides opportunities for new ideas.

The final and perhaps most important point is that local governance is a central feature of the design of the American political system. The benefits of this structural feature are blunted when robust community involvement does not occur. As we noted earlier, it is striking, given the focus on local governance, that Americans distrust authority – even local government and police authority –

more than many other Western democracies. And that distrust undermines the potential gains of local governance. Efforts to bring communities into systems of comanagement are one important way to try to capture the potential of shared decision-making.

7 Conclusion

The goal of this Element was to present a theory-driven and evidence-informed alternative to the current style and culture of policing in America. Legitimacy-based policing, or procedural justice, reimagines the relationship between the police and policed communities. In contrast to traditional carceral policing it offers an equally effective way to address crime while simultaneously building trust and promoting community vitality. In this Element, the evidence is clear and compelling. The same gains in law abidingness can be achieved through a trust-based approach; the police can both ensure public safety and build partnerships with the community. Change can occur within the current structure of policing, but it requires a reimagining of mission, culture, and training.

Within this framework, the views of the public concerning how the police should behave become central to the policies and practices embraced by the latter. When the public believe that the police exercise their authority by carrying out just procedures they view the police as legitimate, and people become more willing to defer to and cooperate with the police in their communities. In the past decade, procedural justice has become a particularly important idea because it offers detailed and specific information about how the police can establish and maintain their legitimacy within communities. The highpoint of this shift is the incorporation of these ideas, in 2015, in President Obama's Task Force on 21st Century Policing. The Task Force represented a period during which the police responded to public concerns by increasing their focus on how to create and maintain public trust and confidence.

Both traditional carceral policing and legitimacy-based policing are found by researchers to lower the crime rate. However, they do so in different ways. Legitimacy-based policing functions through building a more accepting and supportive view of the police among members of the community. This style emphasizes a focus on the experience of the people being policed. People need to feel listened to, to understand why the police act as they do, to feel respected, and to trust that the police are concerned about their issues and concerns. When people have this experience of the police their trust increases. This leads directly to less crime since people are more likely to accept legal authority as legitimate.

The deterrence or "warrior" culture of American policing trains officers to approach problems primarily through the lens of using force to compel compliance. Studies of what the police actually do suggest that this skill set is central to around 4 percent of the tasks that the police perform during most of their working hours. However you look at it, most police work does not require an armed response by a person trained and equipped to deploy force. The situation we find ourselves in today is that America has a narrowly focused police force that is not scaled or trained appropriately to manage the reality of the problems they face. Because America has continually retreated from the task of providing social services in urban communities, the police increasingly deal with a wide variety of incidents – ranging from managing everyday disorder and domestic disputes to dealing with homelessness and mental illness – for which an armed police officer trained to deploy force to obtain coerced compliance is not a desirable solution. The police is increasingly the default agency for dealing with a range of social issues and urban problems for which it is not trained and at which it is not particularly effective.

The warrior model is not only a problem because it equips the police badly for what they actually do most of the time; it is also a problem for police relationships within the wider population. The warrior model does not build public support for the police, either among those they deal with or the broader population. It is not intrinsic to policing to police in a warrior style and, in fact, it is not something that has been true of the police throughout American history. It is a style that became more dominant during an earlier era of high crime.

At present, crime levels in the United States are low compared to the 1990s, so the possibility of repurposing police officers in ways that better enable them to perform the social service tasks that are an increasing component of their everyday activities has increased. Shifting toward a service culture and emphasizing procedural justice can allow the police to more easily provide such services to their communities.

A switch toward legitimacy-based policing is also desirable for the police themselves. One of the by-products of the coercive model of policing is stress on police officers. In America, policing is a career associated with high levels of stress, leading to a wide variety of health and well-being problems for officers who suffer from hypertension and other physical illnesses. They also have high rates of depression, suicide, alcoholism and drug use. You might say that this is all a necessary by-product of doing a tough job, but that is not true. Research suggests that it is more connected to the *style* of policing rather than the job itself.

The current controversy regarding policing and crime mirrors past discussions of policing in that it focuses on the goal of suppressing crime in the moment rather than on creating and implementing a framework to accomplish the long-term goal of addressing the antecedents of crime. The legitimacy-based policing model has the additional advantage that, if adopted, results in a style of policing that both promotes public safety and facilitates the factors within communities that underlie social, political, and economic development. An important advantage of the legitimacy-based policing model is that the promotion of community development can occur within the current structure of policing and requires only a change in police culture to support a service-oriented model.

Once the idea of responsive policing that is shaped by public views becomes central to policing culture, it becomes easy to recognize and address the goal of creating better models through which communities can develop their own capacities to identify their needs and subsequently cooperate with local government agencies, including the police, to identify and implement strategies for managing social order in communities.

What is the benefit of this broader perspective on community goals and increased efforts to involve the community in policing? Taken together, these ideas encourage a reconceptualization of authority relations in our democratic society that begins with the task of identifying and moving beyond the limits of the coercive model. Local institutions and their policies and practices are founded on the consent of the public. Fostering such consent empowers and engages community residents and furthers efforts, such as the development of social capital, reinforce the capacity of communities to determine and enact their own goals.

As noted, this approach does not lack challenges. Communities are disorganized, have competing priorities, and may find it difficult to sustain the forces of development. However, to some extent, these limitations are the result of the general exclusion of communities from authentic shared governance during the coercive era. The greater inclusion of communities itself creates the opportunity to build more vital communities. It also leads to risks that must be managed through the coproduction of social order by the community and local government authorities, including the police.

This Element highlights the advantages of legitimacy-based policing and invites readers to embrace this model. It offers the possibility of "building our way out of crime" – by enhancing the economic, political, and social vitality of communities and the well-being of community residents. When people view the police as legitimate they engage in their communities and that engagement leads to development. The positive influence of trust in the police on *identification with* and *involvement in* communities is shown in research and suggests that the police can play an important role not only in harm reduction but in development, helping communities to join together and address their problems.

Since 2015, unified national pressure to adopt new models of policing has ebbed – and changes in policing, while ongoing, are more scattered and local in nature. Our purpose in this Element is to highlight the argument that, even if political pressures no longer compel the police to adopt legitimacy-based policing, there are still good reasons for them to do so. Those reasons include benefits to both the police and policed communities.

Historically, policing is a crisis-responsive institution, which alters its goals and practices in response to the events that occur in any given era. The present day is no exception to this.

Our goal is to avoid being caught up in the politics of the moment. We believe that reform is often defeated before it begins because it accepts the assumptions of the current system and implements minor tweaks without questioning the existing framework as a whole. Our goal is to present a new theoretical framework that, if adopted, means that the totality of the system can be reimagined.

Finally, we use this Element to highlight the benefits that can flow from drawing upon social science theories when designing law and the policies and practices of legal authority. In this case, the ideas of legitimacy and procedural justice were incorporated by police authorities into their discussions of how to address public concerns about policing. They provided a new and, as it turns out, valuable way of thinking about the goals of policing and the tactics needed to achieve them. Beyond the immediate issues of policing, this is a case study in the utility of social science in the design of law and legal institutions.

References

Abt, T., Bocanegra, E., & Tingirides, E. (2022, December 1). Violent crime in the U.S. is surging. But we know what to do about it. *Time*. https://time.com/6138650/violent-crime-us-surging-what-to-do/.

Aiello, M. F. (2021). Procedural justice and demographic diversity: A quasi-experimental study of police recruitment. *Police Quarterly, 25*(3), 387–411. https://doi.org/10.1177/10986111211043473.

Alexander, L. T. (2012). Hip-hop and housing: Revisiting culture, urban space, power, and law. *Hastings Law Journal, 63*, 803–865.

Ang, D., & Tebes, J. (2021). Civic responses to police violence. Working paper, Kennedy School of Government. https://bit.ly/3FPhqem.

Bailey, T., Dafoe, J., Briere-Godbout, L., & Wang, M. (2016). The new seven majors: Proposed indicator variables to include in the neighborhood stat meter. Unpublished paper, Yale Law School.

Barrett-Howard, E., & Tyler, T. R. (1986). Procedural justice as a criterion in allocation decisions. *Journal of Personality and Social Psychology, 50*(2), 296–304. https://doi.org/10.1037/0022-3514.50.2.296.

Becker, G. S. (1968). Crime and punishment: An economic approach. *Journal of Political Economy, 76*(2), 169–217. https://doi.org/10.1086/259394.

Beckett, K. (2016). The uses and abuses of police discretion: Toward harm reduction policing. *Harvard Law and Policy Review, 10*, 77–100.

Bell, M. C. (2016). Situational trust: How disadvantaged mothers reconceive legal cynicism. *Law & Society Review, 50*(2), 314–347. https://doi.org/10.1111/lasr.12200.

Bell, M. C. (2021). Next-generation policing research: Three propositions. *Journal of Economic Perspectives, 35*(4), 29–48. https://doi.org/10.1257/jep.35.4.29.

Bingham, L. B (2008) Designing justice: Legal institutions and other systems for managing conflict. *Ohio State Journal on Dispute Resolution, 24*(1), 1–51.

Bjerk, R. S. (2022). Does greater police funding help catch more murderers? *Journal of Empirical Legal Studies, 19*(3), 528–559.

Blader, S. L., & Tyler, T. R. (2003). A four-component model of procedural justice: Defining the meaning of a "fair" process. *Personality and Social Psychology Bulletin, 29*(6), 747–758. https://doi.org/10.1177/0146167203029006007.

Bohman, J., & Rehg, W. (1997). *Deliberative democracy: Essays on reason and politics*. MIT Press.

Bolger, P. C., & Walters, G. D. (2019). The relationship between police procedural justice, police legitimacy, and people's willingness to cooperate with law enforcement: A meta-analysis. *Journal of Criminal Justice, 60*, 93–99. https://doi.org/10.1016/j.jcrimjus.2019.01.001.

Bouie, J. (2022, March 3). Biden says "fund the police": Well, they aren't exactly hurting for cash. *New York Times.* https://nyti.ms/3MbAZ1t.

Braga, A. A., & Weisburd, D. L. (2010). *Policing problem places: Crime hot spots and effective prevention.* Oxford University Press.

Brayne, S. (2014). Surveillance and system avoidance: Criminal justice contact and institutional attachment. *American Sociological Review, 79*(3), 367–391. https://doi.org/10.1177/0003122414530398.

Brenan, M. (2021a, July 14). Americans' confidence in major U.S. institutions dips. *Gallup.* https://bit.ly/3T9l3ig.

Brenan, M. (2021b, September 9). Americans' trust in government remains low. *Gallup.* https://bit.ly/3CwrFCg.

Brown, K. L., & Reisig, M. D. (2019). Procedural injustice, police legitimacy, and officer gender: A vignette-based test of the invariance thesis. *Behavioral Sciences & the Law, 37*(6), 696–710. https://doi.org/10.1002/bsl.2439.

Bump, P. (2020, June 7). Over the past 60 years, more spending on police hasn't necessarily meant less crime. *Washington Post.* https://wapo.st/3yfP5Jm.

Camp, N. P., Voigt, R., Jurafsky, D., & Eberhardt, J. L. (2021). The thin blue waveform: Racial disparities in officer prosody undermine institutional trust in the police. *Journal of Personality and Social Psychology, 121*(6), 1157–1171. https://doi.org/10.1037/pspa0000270.

Canadian Index of Wellbeing. (2016). *How are Canadians really doing? The 2016 CIW National report.* Canadian Index of Wellbeing, University of Waterloo.

Canales, R. (2022a). Assessing the effectiveness of procedural justice training for police officers: Evidence from the Mexico City police. Unpublished paper.

Canales, R. (2022b). Evaluation of the Oakland police reform effort. Unpublished paper.

Canales, R. (2022c). Evaluation of the Stockton police reform effort. Unpublished paper.

Chalfin, A., & McCrary, J. (2017). Criminal deterrence: A review of the literature. *Journal of Economic Literature, 55*(1), 5–48. https://doi.org/10.1257/jel.20141147.

Chalfin, A., & McCrary, J. (2018). Are US cities underpoliced? Theory and evidence. *Review of Economics and Statistics, 100*(1), 167–186. https://doi.org/10.1162/REST_a_00694.

Cheng, T. (2020). Input without influence: The silence and scripts of police and community relations. *Social Problems, 67*(1), 171–189. https://doi.org/10.1093/socpro/spz007.

Clifasefi, S. L., Lonczak, H. S., & Collins, S. E. (2017). Seattle's law enforcement assisted diversion (LEAD) program: Within-subjects changes on housing, employment, and income/benefits outcomes and associations with recidivism. *Crime & Delinquency, 63*(4), 429–445. https://doi.org/10.1177/0011128716687550.

Cohen-Charash, Y., & Spector, P. E. (2001). The role of justice in organizations: A meta-analysis. *Organizational Behavior and Human Decision Processes, 86*(2), 278–321. https://doi.org/10.1006/obhd.2001.2958.

Colquitt, J. A., Conlon, D. E., Wesson, M. J., Porter, C. O. L. H., & Ng, K. Y. (2001). Justice at the millennium: A meta-analytic review of 25 years of organizational justice research. *Journal of Applied Psychology, 86*(3), 425–445. https://doi.org/10.1037/0021-9010.86.3.425.

Colquitt, J. A., Scott, B. A., Rodell, J. B., et al. (2013). Justice at the millennium, a decade later: A meta-analytic test of social exchange and affect-based perspectives. *Journal of Applied Psychology, 98*(2), 199–236. https://doi.org/10.1037/a0031757.

Curato, N., Dryzek, J. S., Ercan, S. A., Hendriks, C. M., & Niemeyer, S. (2017). Twelve key findings in deliberative democracy research. *Daedalus, 146*(3), 28–38. https://doi.org/10.1162/DAED_a_00444.

Curran, B. (1977). *The legal needs of the public.* American Bar Foundation.

Currie, A. (2009, May 12). The legal problems of everyday life. Research and Statistics Division, Department of Justice, Canada.

Dai, M., Frank, J., & Sun, I. (2011). Procedural justice during police-citizen encounters: The effects of process-based policing on citizen compliance and demeanor. *Journal of Criminal Justice, 39*(2), 159–168. https://doi.org/10.1016/j.jcrimjus.2011.01.004.

Desmond, M., Papachristos, A. V., & Kirk, D. S. (2016). Police violence and citizen crime reporting in the black community. *American Sociological Review, 81*(5), 857–876. https://doi.org/10.1177/0003122416663494.

Desmond-Harris, J. (2015, April 14). Are black communities overpoliced or underpoliced? Both. *Vox Media.* www.vox.com/2015/4/14/8411733/black-community-policing-crime.

de Tocqueville, A. (2000). *Democracy in America.* Translated by H. C. Mansfield & D. Wintrop. University of Chicago Press.

Dickson, E. S., Gordon, S. C., & Huber, G. A. (2022). Identifying legitimacy: Experimental evidence on compliance with authority. *Science Advances, 8*(7), eabj7377. https://doi.org/10.1126/sciadv.abj7377.

Donner, C. M., Maskaly, J., Fridell, L., & Jennings, W. G. (2015). Policing and procedural justice. *Policing, 38*, 153–172.

Dorf, M., & Sabel, C. (1998). A constitution of democratic experimentalism. *Cornell Law Faculty Publications, 98*(2), 267–473. https://doi.org/10.2307/1123411.

Dryzek, J. S., Bachtiger, A., Chambers, S., et al. (2019). The crisis of democracy and the science of deliberation. *Science, 363*, 1144–1146.

Earley, P. C., & Lind, E. A. (1987). Procedural justice and participation in task selection: The role of control in mediating justice judgments. *Journal of Personality and Social Psychology, 52*(6), 1148–1160. https://doi.org/10.1037/0022-3514.52.6.1148.

Epp, C. R., Maynard-Moody, S., & Haidt-Markel, D. P. (2014). *Pulled over: How police stops define race and citizenship.* University of Chicago Press.

Evans, R., & Farmer, C. (2021). *Do police need guns?* Springer.

Farmer, C., & Evans, R. (2020). Primed and ready: Does arming police increase safety? Preliminary findings. *Violence and Gender, 7*(2), 47–56. https://doi.org/10.1089/vio.2019.0020.

Farrell, D. M., O'Malley, E., & Suiter, J. (2013). Deliberative democracy in action Irish-style: The 2011 *We the Citizens* pilot citizens' assembly. *Irish Political Studies, 28*(1), 99–113. https://doi.org/10.1080/07907184.2012.745274.

Farrington, D. P., Cohn, E. G., & Skinner, G. C. M. (2022). Changes in the most cited scholars in five international journals between 2006 and 2020. *Asian Journal of Criminology, 17*(2), 193–212. https://doi.org/10.1007/s11417-022-09362-x.

Fishkin, J. S. (1991). *Democracy and deliberation.* Yale University Press.

Flippin, M., Reisig, M. D., & Trinkner, R. (2019). The effect of procedural injustice during emergency 911 calls: A factorial vignette-based study. *Journal of Experimental Criminology, 15*(4), 651–660. https://doi.org/10.1007/s11292-019-09369-y.

Folmer, C. R., Kuiper, M., Olthuis, E., et al. (2021). Compliance in the 1.5 meter society: Longitudinal analysis of citizens' adherence to COVID-19 mitigation measures in a representative sample in the Netherlands. *PsyArXiv.* https://doi.org/10.31234/osf.io/dr9q3.

Forman, J. (2017). *Locking up our own: Crime and punishment in black America.* Farrar, Straus and Giroux.

French Jr., J. R. P., & Raven, B. H. (1959). The bases of social power. In D. Cartwright (ed.), *Studies in social power* (pp. 150–167). Institute for Social Research.

Frijters, P., & Krekel, C. (2021). *A handbook of well-being policy making: History, measurement, implementation and examples*. Oxford University Press.

Fung, A. (2004). *Empowered participation: Reinventing urban democracy*. Princeton University Press.

Geller, W. A., & Toch, H. (1959). *Police violence: Understanding and controlling police abuse of force*. Yale University Press.

Goff, P. A., & Tyler, T. R. (2018). Public views about the police: The results of a national survey. National Opinion Research Center, University of Chicago.

Goff, P. A., Swencionis, J. K., & Tyler, T. R. (2022). Social attitudes, not fear of crime, shape public support for coercive criminal law policies. Unpublished manuscript.

Gohara, M. (2022). Black survivors' visions for justice. Unpublished manuscript.

Gold, M. E. (1999). *The complete social scientist: A Kurt Lewin reader*. American Psychological Association Press.

Gordon, D. (2022). *Policing the racial divide: Urban growth politics and the remaking of segregation*. New York University Press.

Gramlich, J. (2020, November 21). What the data says (and doesn't say) about crime in the United States. Pew Research Center. https://bit.ly/3VFqQi3.

Grönlund, K., Setälä, M., & Herne, K. (2010). Deliberation and civic virtue: Lessons from a citizen deliberation experiment. *European Political Science Review, 2*(1), 95–117. https://doi.org/10.1017/S1755773909990245.

Habermas, J. (1989). *The structural transformation of the public sphere*. Polity Press.

Hagan, J., & Hans, V. (2017). Procedural justice theory and public policy. *Annual Review of Law and Social Science, 13*, 1–3.

Hamilton, M. (2018). Understanding what shapes varying perceptions of the procedural fairness of transboundary environmental decision-making processes. *Ecology and Society, 23*(4), 48. https://doi.org/10.5751/ES-10625-230448.

Hartley, T. A., Burchfiel, C. M., Fekedulegn, D., Andrew, M. E., & Violanti, J. M. (2011). Health disparities in police officers: Comparisons to the U.S. general population. *International Journal of Emergency Mental Health, 13*(4), 211–220.

Held, D. (2006). *Models of democracy*. Stanford University Press.

Herbert, S. (2006). *Citizens, cops, and power*. University of Chicago Press.

Higgins, A. (2019). *Understanding the public's priorities for policing*. The Police Foundation.

Hough, M., Jackson, J., & Bradford, B. (2013). Legitimacy, trust, and compliance: An empirical test of procedural justice theory using the European social survey.

In J. Tankebe & A. Liebling (eds.), *Legitimacy and criminal justice: An international exploration* (pp. 326–352). Oxford University Press.

Hunt, D. E. (1987). *Beginning with ourselves*. Brookline Books.

Hunter, M. A. (2010). The nightly round: Space, social capital, and urban black nightlife. *City & Community, 9*(2), 165–186. https://doi.org/10.1111/j.1540-6040.2010.01320.x.

Hunter, M. A., Pattillo, M., Robinson, Z. F., & Taylor, K.-Y. (2016). Black placemaking: Celebration, play, and poetry. *Theory, Culture & Society, 33*(7–8), 31–56. https://doi.org/10.1177/0263276416635259.

Huo, Y. J. (2002). Justice and the regulation of social relations. *British Journal of Social Psychology, 41*, 535–562.

Huq, A., Tyler, T., & Schulhofer, S. (2011). Mechanisms for eliciting cooperation in counterterrorism policing: Evidence from the United Kingdom. *Journal of Empirical Legal Studies, 8*(4), 728–761. https://doi.org/10.1111/j.1740-1461.2011.01239.x.

Jackson, J. (2018). Norms, normativity, and the legitimacy of justice institutions: International perspectives. *Annual Review of Law and Social Science, 14*(1), 145–165. https://doi.org/10.1146/annurev-lawsocsci-110316-113734.

Jackson, J., Bradford, B., Stanko, E. A., & Hohl, K. (2012). *Just authority? Trust in the police in England and Wales*. Routledge.

Jonathan-Zamir, T., Perry, G., & Weisburd, D. (2020). Illuminating the concept of community (group)-level procedural justice: A qualitative analysis of protestors' group-level experiences with the police. *Criminal Justice and Behavior, 48*(6), 791–809. https://doi.org/10.1177/0093854820983388.

Kaase, M. (1999). Interpersonal trust, political trust and non-institutionalised political participation in Western Europe. *West European Politics, 22*(3), 1–21. https://doi.org/10.1080/01402389908425313.

Karimi, F., & Lemos, G. (2021, October 29). Fights erupted at a high school in Louisiana. So these dads took matters in their own hands. *CNN*. https://cnn.it/3Dc0rB1.

Katz, B., & Nowak, J. (2018). *The new localism: How cities can thrive in an age of populism*. Brookings Institution.

Keizer, K., Lindenberg, S., & Steg, L. (2008). The spreading of disorder. *Science, 322*(5908), 1681–1685. https://doi.org/10.1126/science.1161405.

Kelley, H. H., & Stahelski, A. J. (1970). Social interaction basis of cooperators' and competitors' belief about others. *Journal of Personality and Social Psychology, 16*, 66–91.

Kelling, G. L. & Wilson, J. Q. (1982). Broken windows. *Atlantic Monthly, 249*, 29–38.

Kellstedt, P. M., Zahran, S., & Vedlitz, A. (2008). Personal efficacy, the information environment, and attitudes toward global warming and climate change in the United States. *Risk Analysis, 28*(1), 113–126. https://doi.org/10.1111/j.1539-6924.2008.01010.x.

Kelman, H., & Hamilton, V. L. (1989). *Crimes of obedience: Toward a social psychology of authority and responsibility.* Yale University Press.

Kim, Y., Kee, Y., & Lee, S. J. (2015). An analysis of the relative importance of components in measuring community wellbeing: Perspectives of citizens, public officials, and experts. *Social Indicators Research, 121*(2), 345–369. https://doi.org/10.1007/s11205-014-0652-4.

Kirkpatrick, D. D., Eder, S., Barker, K., & Tate, J. (2021, October 21). Officers, trained to presume danger, have reacted with outsize aggression. For hundreds of unarmed drivers, the consequences have been fatal. *New York Times.*

Kleiman, M. A. R. (2009). *When brute force fails: How to have less crime and less punishment.* Princeton University Press.

Kochel, T. R. (2012). Can police legitimacy promote collective efficacy? *Justice Quarterly, 29*(3), 384–419. https://doi.org/10.1080/07418825.2011.561805.

Kooistra, E. B., Folmer, C. R., Kuiper, M. E., et al. (2021). Mitigating COVID-19 in a nationally representative UK sample: Personal abilities and obligation to obey the law shape compliance with mitigation measures. *PsyArXiv.* https://doi.org/10.31234/osf.io/zuc23.

Krauss, D. A., Cook, G. I., Song, E., & Umanath, S. (2021). The public's perception of crime control theater laws: It's complicated. *Psychology, Public Policy, and Law, 27*(3), 316–327. https://doi.org/10.1037/law0000302.

Krauss, D. A., Cook, G. I., Umanath, S., & Song, E. (2022). Changing the public's crime control theater attitudes. *Psychology, Public Policy, and Law.* https://doi.org/10.1037/law0000340.

Krekel, C., De Neve, J.-E., Fancourt, D., & Layard, R. (2021). A local community course that raises wellbeing and pro-sociality: Evidence from a randomised controlled trial. *Journal of Economic Behavior & Organization, 188*, 322–336. https://doi.org/10.1016/j.jebo.2021.05.021.

Kyprianides, A., Bradford, B., Jackson, J., Stott, C., & Pósch, K. (2021). Relational and instrumental perspectives on compliance with the law among people experiencing homelessness. *Law and Human Behavior, 46*(1), 1–14. https://doi.org/10.1037/lhb0000465.

Lacey, J., Edwards, P., & Lamont, J. (2016). Social licence as social contract: Procedural fairness and forest agreement-making in Australia. *Forestry, 89*(5), 489–499. https://doi.org/10.1093/forestry/cpw027.

Lanfear, C. C., Matsueda, R. L., & Beach, L. R. (2020). Broken windows, informal social control, and crime: Assessing causality in empirical studies.

Annual Review of Criminology, 3(1), 97–120. https://doi.org/10.1146/annurev-criminol-011419-041541.

Lavoie, J. A. A., Alvarez, N., & Kandil, Y. (2022). Developing community co-designed scenario-based training for police mental health crisis response: A relational policing approach to de-escalation. *Journal of Police and Criminal Psychology, 37*(3), 587–601. https://doi.org/10.1007/s11896-022-09500-2.

Leary, M. R. (2007). Motivational and emotional aspects of the self. *Annual Review of Psychology, 58*(1), 317–344. https://doi.org/10.1146/annurev.psych.58.110405.085658.

Lerman, A. E., & Weaver, V. M. (2014). *Arresting citizenship: The democratic consequences of American crime control.* University of Chicago Press.

Leventhal, G. S. (1980). What should be done with equity theory? New approaches to the study of fairness in social relationships. In K. J. Gergen, M. S. Greenberg, & R. H. Willis (eds.), *Social exchange* (pp. 27–55). Plenum Press.

Levine, J. R. (2016). The privatization of political representation: Community-based organizations as nonelected neighborhood representatives. *American Sociological Review, 81*(6), 1251–1275. https://doi.org/10.1177/0003122416670655.

Lewin, K., Lippitt, R., & White, R. K. (1939). Patterns of aggressive behavior in experimentally created "social climates." *Journal of Social Psychology, 10*(2), 269–299. https://doi.org/10.1080/00224545.1939.9713366.

Lind, E. A., & Lissak, R. I. (1985). Apparent impropriety and procedural fairness judgments. *Journal of Experimental Social Psychology, 21*(1), 19–29. https://doi.org/10.1016/0022-1031(85)90003-4.

Lind, E. A., & Tyler, T. R. (1988). *The social psychology of procedural justice.* Plenum Press.

Lorenzoni, I., & Pidgeon, N. F. (2006). Public views on climate change: European and USA perspectives. *Climatic Change, 77*(1), 73–95. https://doi.org/10.1007/s10584-006-9072-z.

Lubell, M., Vedlitz, A., Zahran, S., & Alston, L. T. (2006). Collective action, environmental activism, and air quality policy. *Political Research Quarterly, 59*(1), 149–160. https://doi.org/10.1177/106591290605900113.

Lum, C., Koper, C. S., & Wu, X. (2021). Can we really defund the police? A nine-agency study of police response to calls for service. *Police Quarterly, 25*(3), 255–280. https://doi.org/10.1177/10986111211035002.

MacCoun, R. J. (2005). Voice, control, and belonging: The double-edged sword of procedural fairness. *Annual Review of Law and Social Science, 1*(1), 171–201. https://doi.org/10.1146/annurev.lawsocsci.1.041604.115958.

MacDonald, J. M., Manz, P. W., Alpert, G. P., & Dunham, R. G. (2003). Police use of force: Examining the relationship between calls for service and the balance of police force and suspect resistance. *Journal of Criminal Justice, 31*(2), 119–127. https://doi.org/10.1016/S0047-2352 (02)00219-2.

Mastrofski, S. D., Snipes, J. B., & Supina, A. E. (1996). Compliance on demand: The public's response to specific police requests. *Journal of Research in Crime and Delinquency, 33*(3), 269–305. https://doi.org/10.1177/0022427896033003001.

Mazerolle, L., Bennett, S., Antrobus, E., & Eggins, E. (2012). Procedural justice, routine encounters and citizen perceptions of police: Main findings from the Queensland Community Engagement Trial (QCET). *Journal of Experimental Criminology, 8*(4), 343–367. https://doi.org/10.1007/s11292-012-9160-1.

Mazerolle, L., Antrobus, E., Bennett, S., & Tyler, T. R. (2013a). Shaping citizen perceptions of police legitimacy: A randomized field trial of procedural justice. *Criminology, 51*(1), 33–63. https://doi.org/10.1111/j.1745-9125.2012.00289.x.

Mazerolle, L., Bennett, S., Davis, J., Sargeant, E., & Manning, M. (2013b). Procedural justice and police legitimacy: A systematic review of the research evidence. *Journal of Experimental Criminology, 9*(3), 245–274. https://doi.org/10.1007/s11292-013-9175-2.

Mazerolle, L., Sargeant, E., Cherney, A., et al. (2014). *Procedural justice and legitimacy in policing*. Springer.

McCluskey, J. D. (2003). *Police requests for compliance: Coercive and pro-cedurally just tactics*. LFB Scholarship Publishing.

McCluskey, J. D., Mastrofski, S. D., & Parks, R. B. (1999). To acquiesce or rebel: Predicting citizen compliance with police requests. *Police Quarterly, 2*(4), 389–416. https://doi.org/10.1177/109861119900200401.

McIntire, M., & Keller, M. H. (2021, October 31). The demand for money behind many police traffic stops. *New York Times*. www.nytimes.com/2021/10/31/us/police-ticket-quotas-money-funding.html.

Milgram, S. (1975). *Obedience to authority: An experimental view*. Harper Colophon.

Miller, D. T. (2001). Disrespect and the experience of injustice. *Annual Review of Psychology, 52*(1), 527–553. https://doi.org/10.1146/annurev.psych.52.1.527.

Muir, W. K. (1979). *Police: Streetcorner politicians*. University of Chicago Press.

Mumford, E. A., Liu, W., & Taylor, B. G. (2021). Profiles of U.S. law enforcement officers' physical, psychological, and behavioral health: Results from a nationally representative survey of officers. *Police Quarterly, 24*(3), 357–381. https://doi.org/10.1177/1098611121991111.

Mummolo, J. (2018). Militarization fails to enhance police safety or reduce crime but may harm police reputation. *Proceedings of the National Academy of Sciences of the United States of America, 115*(37), 9181–9186. https://doi.org/10.1073/pnas.1805161115.

Murphy, K., & McCarthy, M. (2022). Confirming or resisting the "racist cop" stereotype?: The importance of a police officer's "guardian" identity in moderating support for procedural justice. *Psychology, Crime & Law.* https://doi.org/10.1080/1068316X.2022.2043314

Murphy, K., Williamson, H., Sargeant, E., & McCarthy, M. (2020). Why people comply with COVID-19 social distancing restrictions: Self-interest or duty? *Australian & New Zealand Journal of Criminology, 53*(4), 477–496. https://doi.org/10.1177/0004865820954484.

Murphy, K., Bradford, B., Sargeant, E., & Cherney, A. (2022). Building immigrants' solidarity with police: Procedural justice, identity and immigrants' willingness to cooperate with police. *British Journal of Criminology, 62*(2), 299–319. https://doi.org/10.1093/bjc/azab052.

Nägel, C., & Vera, A. (2021). More cops, less trust? Disentangling the relationship between police numbers and trust in the police in the European Union. *Policing: A Journal of Policy and Practice, 15*(2), 939–949. https://doi.org/10.1093/police/paaa098.

Nivette, A., Nagel, C., & Stan, A. (2022). The use of experimental vignettes in studying police procedural justice: A systematic Review. *Journal of Experimental Criminology.* https://doi.org/10.1007/s11292-022-09529-7.

O'Brien, D. T., Farrell, C., & Welsh, B. C. (2019). Looking through broken windows: The impact of neighborhood disorder on aggression and fear of crime is an artifact of research design. *Annual Review of Criminology, 2*(1), 53–71. https://doi.org/10.1146/annurev-criminol-011518-024638.

O'Brien, T. C., Tyler, T. R., & Meares, T. L. (2019). Building popular legitimacy with reconciliatory gestures and participation: A community-level model of authority. *Regulation & Governance, 14*(4), 821–839. https://doi.org/10.1111/rego.12264.

Owens, E., & Ba, B. (2021). The economics of policing and public safety. *Journal of Economic Perspectives, 35*(4), 3–28. https://doi.org/10.1257/jep.35.4.3.

Parker, K., & Hurst, K. (2021, October 26). Growing share of Americans say they want more spending on police in their area. Pew Research Center. https://pewrsr.ch/3seecZY.

Parker, K. F. (2015). The African-American entrepreneur–crime drop relationship: Growing African-American business ownership and declining youth violence. *Urban Affairs Review, 51*(6), 751–780. https://doi.org/10.1177/1078087415571755.

Parkinson, J., & Mansbridge, J. (2012). *Deliberative systems: Deliberative democracy at the large scale.* Cambridge University Press.

Parks, R. B., Mastrofski, S. D., DeJong, C., & Gray, M. K. (1999). How officers spend their time with the community. *Justice Quarterly, 16*(3), 483–518. https://doi.org/10.1080/07418829900094241.

Peyton, K., Sierra-Arévalo, M., & Rand, D. G. (2019). A field experiment on community policing and police legitimacy. *Proceedings of the National Academy of Sciences of the United States of America, 116*(40), 19894–19898. https://doi.org/10.1073/pnas.1910157116.

Phillips, R., & Wong, C. (2017). *Handbook of community well-being research.* Springer.

Pina-Sánchez, J., & Brunton-Smith, I. (2020). Reassessing the relationship between procedural justice and police legitimacy. *Law and Human Behavior, 44*(5), 377–393. https://doi.org/10.1037/lhb0000424.

Piza, E. L., & Sytsma, V. A. (2022). The impact of suspect resistance, informational justice, and interpersonal justice on time until police use of physical force: A survival analysis. *Crime & Delinquency, 0*(0). https://doi.org/10.1177/00111287221106947.

Poortinga, W., & Pidgeon, N. F. (2003). Exploring the dimensionality of trust in risk regulation. *Risk Analysis, 23*(5), 961–972. https://doi.org/10.1111/1539-6924.00373.

Prowse, G., Weaver, V. M., & Meares, T. L. (2019). The state from below: Distorted responsiveness in policed communities. *Urban Affairs Review, 56* (5), 1423–1471. https://doi.org/10.1177/1078087419844831.

Quattlebaum, M., & Tyler, T. (2020). Beyond the law: An agenda for policing reform. *Boston University Law Review, 100*, 1017–1046.

Reinders, F. C., Kuiper, M. E., Olthuis, E., et al. (2020). Sustaining compliance with Covid-19 mitigation measures? Understanding distancing behavior in the Netherlands during June 2020. *PsyArXiv.* https://doi.org/10.31234/osf.io/xafwp.

Reisig, M. D., Flippin, M., Meško, G., & Trinkner, R. (2021). The effects of justice judgments on police legitimacy across urban neighborhoods: A test of the invariance thesis. *Crime & Delinquency, 67*(9), 1295–1318. https://doi.org/10.1177/0011128720977435.

Roscigno, V. J., & Preito-Hodge, K. (2021). Racist cops, vested "blue" interests, or both? Evidence from four decades of the General Social Survey. *Socius, 7*, 1–13.

Sampson, R. J., Raudenbush, S. W., & Earls, F. (1997). Neighborhoods and violent crime: A multilevel study of collective efficacy. *Science, 277*(5328), 918–924. https://doi.org/10.1126/science.277.5328.918.

Sandefur, R. L. (2012). Money isn't everything: Understanding moderate income households' use of lawyers' services. In A. Duggan, L. Sossin, & M. Trebilcock (eds.), *Middle income access to justice* (pp. 222–245). University of Toronto Press.

Sandefur, R. L. (2015). Elements of professional expertise: Understanding relational and substantive expertise through lawyers' impact. *American Sociological Review, 80*(5), 909–933. https://doi.org/10.1177/0003122 415601157.

Sargeant, E., Davoren, N., & Murphy, K. (2021). The defiant and the compliant: How does procedural justice theory explain ethnic minority group postures toward police? *Policing and Society, 31*(3), 283–303. https://doi.org/ 10.1080/10439463.2020.1720016.

Scrivens, K., & Smith, C. (2013). Four interpretations of social capital: An agenda for measurement. OECD statistics working paper, no. 2013/06.

Sierra-Arévalo, M. (2021). American policing and the danger imperative. *Law & Society Review, 55*(1), 70–103. https://doi.org/10.1111/lasr.12526.

Sklansky, D. (2014). The promise and perils of police professionalism. In J. M. Brown (ed.), *The Future of Policing* (pp. 343–354). Routledge.

Skogan, W., & Frydl, K. (2004). *Fairness and effectiveness in policing: The EVIDENCE.* National Research Council.

Smith, H. J., Tyler, T. R., Huo, Y. J., Ortiz, D. J., & Lind, E. A. (1998). The self-relevant implications of the group-value model: Group membership, self-worth, and treatment quality. *Journal of Experimental Social Psychology, 34*(5), 470–493. https://doi.org/10.1006/jesp.1998.1360.

Soss, J., & Weaver, V. (2017). Police are our government: Politics, political science, and the policing of race–class subjugated communities. *Annual Review of Political Science, 20*(1), 565–591. https://doi.org/10.1146/ annurev-polisci-060415-093825.

Spade, D. (2020). *Mutual aid: Building solidarity during this crisis.* Verso.

Stoughton, S. W. (2014). Policing facts. *Tulane Law Review, 88*, 847–898.

Stromberg, J. (2015, February 27). Firefighters do a lot less firefighting than they used to. Here's what they do instead. *Vox.* www.vox.com/2014/10/30/ 7079547/fire-firefighter-decline-medical.

Sunshine, J., & Tyler, T. R. (2003). The role of procedural justice and legitimacy in shaping public support for policing. *Law & Society Review, 37*(3), 513–548. https://doi.org/10.1111/1540-5893.3703002.

Tajfel, H., & Turner, J. C. (1986). The social identity theory of intergroup behaviour. In W. G. Austin & S. Worchel (eds.), *Psychology of intergroup relations* (pp. 7–24). Nelson-Hall.

Tankebe, J. (2009). Public cooperation with the police in Ghana: Does procedural fairness matter? *Criminology, 47*(4), 1265–1293. https://doi.org/10.1111/j.1745-9125.2009.00175.x.

Terrill, W. (2001). *Police coercion: Application of the force continuum.* LFB Scholarly Publishing.

Terrill, W., Rossler, M. T., & Paoline III, E. A. (2014). Police service delivery and responsiveness in a period of economic instability. *Police Practice and Research, 15*(6), 490–504. https://doi.org/10.1080/15614263.2013.829606.

Thibaut, J., & Kelley, H. H. (1959). *The social psychology of groups.* Wiley.

Thibaut, J., & Walker, L. (1975). *Procedural justice: A psychological analysis.* Erlbaum.

Trinkner, R., Tyler, T. R., & Goff, P. A. (2016). Justice from within: The relations between a procedurally just organizational climate and police organizational efficiency, endorsement of democratic policing, and officer well-being. *Psychology, Public Policy, and Law, 22*(2), 158–172. https://doi.org/10.1037/law0000085.

Tyler, T. R. (1987). Conditions leading to value-expressive effects in judgments of procedural justice: A test of four models. *Journal of Personality and Social Psychology, 52*(2), 333–344. https://doi.org/10.1037/0022-3514.52.2.333.

Tyler, T. R. (1990). *Why people obey the law.* Yale University Press.

Tyler, T. R. (2006a). Psychological perspectives on legitimacy and legitimation. *Annual Review of Psychology, 57*(1), 375–400. https://doi.org/10.1146/annurev.psych.57.102904.190038.

Tyler, T. R. (2006b). *Why people obey the law.* Princeton University Press.

Tyler, T. R., & Blader, S. L. (2000). *Cooperation in groups: Procedural justice, social identity, and behavioral engagement.* Psychology Press.

Tyler, T. R., & Caine, A. (1981). The influence of outcomes and procedures on satisfaction with formal leaders. *Journal of Personality and Social Psychology, 41*(4), 642–655. https://doi.org/10.1037/0022-3514.41.4.642

Tyler, T. R., & Fagan, J. (2008). Legitimacy and cooperation: Why do people help the police fight crime in their communities. *Ohio State Journal of Criminal Law, 6,* 231–275.

Tyler, T. R., & Huo, Y. (2002). *Trust in the law: Encouraging public cooperation with the police and courts.* Russell Sage Foundation.

Tyler, T. R., & Jackson, J. (2014). Popular legitimacy and the exercise of legal authority: Motivating compliance, cooperation, and engagement. *Psychology, Public Policy, and Law, 20*(1), 78–95. https://doi.org/10.1037/a0034514.

Tyler, T. R., & Lind, E. A. (1992). A relational model of authority in groups. In M. Zanna (ed.), *Advances in experimental social psychology* (pp. 115–191). Academic Press.

Tyler, T. R., & Meares, T. (2021). Revisiting broken windows: The role of the community and the police in promoting community engagement. *NYU Annual Survey of American Law, 76*, 637–656.

Tyler, T. R., & Trinkner, R. (2018). *Why Children Follow Rules*. Oxford University Press.

Tyler, T. R., Boeckmann, R., Smith, H. J., & Huo, Y. J. (1997). *Social justice in a diverse society*. Westview Press.

Tyler, T. R., Fagan, J., & Geller, A. (2014). Street stops and police legitimacy: Teachable moments in young urban men's legal socialization. *Journal of Empirical Legal Studies, 11*(4), 751–785. https://doi.org/10.1111/jels.12055.

Tyler, T. R., Goff, P. A., & MacCoun, R. J. (2015). The impact of psychological science on policing in the United States: Procedural justice, legitimacy, and effective law enforcement. *Psychological Science in the Public Interest, 16*(3), 75–109. https://doi.org/10.1177/1529100615617791.

Tyler, T. R., Jackson, J., & Mentovich, A. (2015). The consequences of being an object of suspicion: Potential pitfalls of proactive police contact. *Journal of Empirical Legal Studies, 12*(4), 602–636. https://doi.org/10.1111/jels.12086.

Van Rooij, B., de Bruijn, A. L., Folmer, C. R., et al. (2021). Compliance with COVID-19 mitigation measures in the United States. *PsyArXiv*. https://doi.org/10.31234/osf.io/qymu3.

Vaughn, P. E., Peyton, K., & Huber, G. A. (2022). Mass support for proposals to reshape policing depends on the implications for crime and safety. *Criminology and Public Policy, 21*, 125–146.

Violanti, J. M., Fekedulegn, D., Hartley, T. A., et al. (2013). Life expectancy in police officers: A comparison with the U.S. general population. *International Journal of Emergency Mental Health, 15*(4), 217–228. https://pubmed.ncbi.nlm.nih.gov/24707585/.

Voigt, R., Camp, N. P., Prabhakaran, V., et al. (2017). Language from police body camera footage shows racial disparities in officer respect. *Proceedings of the National Academy of Sciences of the United States of America, 114*(25), 6521–6526. https://doi.org/10.1073/pnas.1702413114.

Walters, G. D., & Bolger, P. C. (2018). Procedural justice perceptions, legitimacy beliefs, and compliance with the law: A meta-analysis. *Journal of Experimental Criminology, 15*(3), 341–372. https://doi.org/10.1007/s11292-018-9338-2.

Watson, A. C., Compton, M. T., & Pope, L. G. (2019). *Crisis response services for people with mental illnesses or intellectual and developmental disabilities: A review of the literature on police-based and other first response models*. VERA Institute of Justice.

Webster, J. A. (1970). Police time and task study. *Journal of Criminal Law, 61,* 94–100. https://doi.org/10.2307/1142102.

Weisburd, D. (2016). Does hot spots policing inevitably lead to unfair and abusive police practices, or can we maximize both fairness and effectiveness in the new proactive policing? *University of Chicago Legal Forum, 2016,* 661–686.

Weisburd, D., & Majmundar, M. K. (2018). *Proactive policing: Effects on crime and communities.* The National Academies Press.

Weisburd, D., & Neyroud, P. (2011). *Police science: Toward a new paradigm.* Harvard University Press.

Weisburd, D., Telep, C. W., Vovak, H., et al. (2022). Reforming the police through procedural justice training: A multicity randomized trial at crime hot spots. *Proceedings of the National Academy of Sciences of the United States of America, 119*(14), e2118780119. https://doi.org/10.1073/pnas.21187 80119.

Wheelock, D., Stroshine, M. S., & O'Hear, M. (2019). Disentangling the relationship between race and attitudes toward the police: Police contact, perceptions of safety, and procedural justice. *Crime & Delinquency, 65*(7), 941–968. https://doi.org/10.1177/0011128718811928.

Winter, S. C., & May, P. J. (2001). Motivation for compliance with environmental regulations. *Journal of Policy Analysis and Management, 20*(4), 675–698. https://doi.org/10.1002/pam.1023.

Wolfe, S. E., Nix, J., Kaminski, R., & Rojek, J. (2016). Is the effect of procedural justice on police legitimacy invariant? Testing the generality of procedural justice and competing antecedents of legitimacy. *Journal of Quantitative Criminology, 32*(2), 253–282. https://doi.org/10.1007/s10940-015-9263-8.

Wood, G., Tyler, T. R., & Papachristos, A. V. (2020). Procedural justice training reduces police use of force and complaints against officers. *Proceedings of the National Academy of Sciences of the United States of America, 117*(18), 9815–9821. https://doi.org/10.1073/pnas.1920671117.

Yasrebi-De Kom, F. M., Dirkzwager, A. J. E., Van Der Laan, P. H., & Nieuwbeerta, P. (2022). The effect of sanction severity and its interaction with procedural justice. *Criminal Justice and Behavior, 49*(2), 200–219. https://doi.org/10.1177/00938548211038358.

Yesberg, J. A., & Bradford, B. (2021). Policing and collective efficacy: A rapid evidence assessment. *International Journal of Police Science & Management, 23*(4), 417–430. https://doi.org/10.1177/14613557211026938.

Zahnow, R., Mazerolle, L., & Pang, A. (2021). Do individual differences matter in the way people view police legitimacy? A partial replication and extension of invariance thesis. *Policing: A Journal of Policy and Practice, 15*(2), 665–685. https://doi.org/10.1093/police/paz066.

Zimbardo, P. G. (1969). The human choice: Individuation, reason, and order versus deindividuation, impulse, and chaos. *Nebraska Symposium on Motivation, 17,* 237–307.

About the Authors

Tom R. Tyler is trained as a social psychologist. He is the Macklin Fleming Professor of Law and Professor of Psychology at Yale University. His research focuses on authority dynamics in groups, organizations, and societies. He is the author of *Why People Obey the Law*; *Cooperation in Groups; Why People Cooperate; Why Children Follow Rules*; and *Trust in the Law*. In particular, he studies the courts, the police, and prisons. For the last ten years he has been teaching at Yale Law School, were he cofounded the Justice Collaboratory – a research group focused on evidence-informed reforms in criminal justice.

Caroline Nobo is Executive Director of the Justice Collaboratory and a Research Scholar in Law at Yale Law School. Her research as a criminologist focuses on promoting transparency and trust in the criminal legal system. Her expertise includes policing, gun violence, data systems, community-based research methodologies, and the progressive prosecutor movement. She is often featured translating research into policy for broad audiences, in media outlets such as USA Today. Nobo holds a Master in Science in Criminology from the University of Pennsylvania and a B.A. in Sociology from Mount Holyoke College.

Cambridge Elements $^{\equiv}$

Criminology

David Weisburd
George Mason University
Hebrew University of Jerusalem

Advisory Board

About the series

Elements in Criminology seeks to identify key contributions in theory and empirical research that help to identify, enable, and stake out advances in contemporary criminology. The series will focus on radical new ways of understanding and framing criminology, whether of place, communities, persons, or situations. The relevance of criminology for preventing and controlling crime will also be a key focus of this series.

Cambridge Elements

Criminology

Printed in the United States
by Baker & Taylor Publisher Services